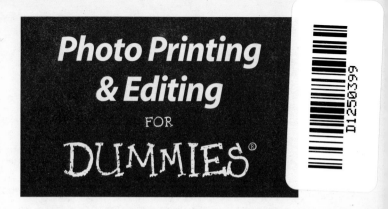

Photo Printing & Editing
FOR
DUMMIES®

Based on *Digital Photography For Dummies,* 4th Edition

by Julie Adair King

WILEY

Wiley Publishing, Inc.

Photo Printing & Editing For Dummies®

Published by
Wiley Publishing, Inc.
111 River Street
Hoboken, NJ 07030-5774

Copyright © 2004 by Wiley Publishing, Inc., Indianapolis, Indiana

Published by Wiley Publishing, Inc., Indianapolis, Indiana

Published simultaneously in Canada

No part of this publication may be reproduced, stored in a retrieval system or transmitted in any form or by any means, electronic, mechanical, photocopying, recording, scanning, or otherwise, except as permitted under Sections 107 or 108 of the 1976 United States Copyright Act, without either the prior written permission of the Publisher, or authorization through payment of the appropriate per-copy fee to the Copyright Clearance Center, 222 Rosewood Drive, Danvers, MA 01923, (978) 750-8400, fax (978) 646-8600. Requests to the Publisher for permission should be addressed to the Legal Department, Wiley Publishing, Inc., 10475 Crosspoint Blvd., Indianapolis, IN 46256, (317) 572-3447, fax (317) 572-4447, e-mail: permcoordinator@wiley.com.

Trademarks: Wiley, the Wiley Publishing logo, For Dummies, the Dummies Man logo, A Reference for the Rest of Us!, The Dummies Way, Dummies Daily, The Fun and Easy Way, Dummies.com, and related trade dress are trademarks or registered trademarks of John Wiley & Sons, Inc. and/or its affiliates in the United States and other countries, and may not be used without written permission. All other trademarks are the property of their respective owners. Wiley Publishing, Inc., is not associated with any product or vendor mentioned in this book.

LIMIT OF LIABILITY/DISCLAIMER OF WARRANTY: WHILE THE PUBLISHER AND AUTHOR HAVE USED THEIR BEST EFFORTS IN PREPARING THIS BOOK, THEY MAKE NO REPRESENTATIONS OR WARRANTIES WITH RESPECT TO THE ACCURACY OR COMPLETENESS OF THE CONTENTS OF THIS BOOK AND SPECIFICALLY DISCLAIM ANY IMPLIED WARRANTIES OF MERCHANTABILITY OR FITNESS FOR A PARTICULAR PURPOSE. NO WARRANTY MAY BE CREATED OR EXTENDED BY SALES REPRESENTATIVES OR WRITTEN SALES MATERIALS. THE ADVICE AND STRATEGIES CONTAINED HEREIN MAY NOT BE SUITABLE FOR YOUR SITUATION. YOU SHOULD CONSULT WITH A PROFESSIONAL WHERE APPROPRIATE. NEITHER THE PUBLISHER NOR AUTHOR SHALL BE LIABLE FOR ANY LOSS OF PROFIT OR ANY OTHER COMMERCIAL DAMAGES, INCLUDING BUT NOT LIMITED TO SPECIAL, INCIDENTAL, CONSEQUENTIAL, OR OTHER DAMAGES.

For general information on our other products and services or to obtain technical support, please contact our Customer Care Department within the U.S. at 800-762-2974, outside the U.S. at 317-572-3993, or fax 317-572-4002.

Wiley also publishes its books in a variety of electronic formats. Some content that appears in print may not be available in electronic books.

ISBN: 0-7645-6783-7

Manufactured in the United States of America

10 9 8 7 6 5 4 3 2 1

1O/RR/QS/QU/IN

WILEY

Publisher's Acknowledgments

We're proud of this book; please send us your comments through our online registration form located at www.dummies.com/register/.

Some of the people who helped bring this book to market include the following:

Acquisitions, Editorial, and Media Development

Project Editor: Jan Withers

Editorial Manager: Rev Mengle

Media Development Manager: Laura VanWinkle

Media Development Supervisor: Richard Graves

Cartoons: Rich Tennant, www.the5thwave.com

Production

Project Coordinator: Jay Kern

Layout and Graphics: Amanda Carter, Carrie Foster, Lynsey Osborn, Jacque Schneider, Melanee Wolven

Proofreaders: Vicki Broyles, Andy Hollandbeck, Dwight Ramsey

Special Help
Kyle Looper

Publishing and Editorial for Technology Dummies

Richard Swadley, Vice President and Executive Group Publisher

Andy Cummings, Vice President and Publisher

Mary C. Corder, Editorial Director

Publishing for Consumer Dummies

Diane Graves Steele, Vice President and Publisher

Joyce Pepple, Acquisitions Director

Composition Services

Gerry Fahey, Vice President of Production Services

Debbie Stailey, Director of Composition Services

Table of Contents

● ●

Introduction

● ●

Digital photography enables you to share visual information with people around the world instantaneously. Literally minutes after snapping a digital picture, you can put the photo in the hands of friends or colleagues near or far by attaching it to an e-mail message or posting it on the World Wide Web. Just as important, digital cameras are *fun*. When was the last time you could say that about a piece of computer equipment?

Like any new technology, digital cameras can be a bit intimidating. Browse the digital camera aisle in your favorite store and you come face-to-face with such technical terms as *pixels, JPEG,* and *ISO.* Don't run — *Photo Printing & Editing For Dummies* explains just what you need to know to become a successful digital photographer, including shooting, editing, and printing your pictures so they look their best.

How to Use This Book

You can read this book in any order that makes sense to you; some chapters provide practical information on choosing a good printer and paper, while others focus on helping you use your digital camera to its best advantage. Or you can turn straight to the user guide in the Bonus Section to start playing with the Digital Photos For Dummies software right away!

How This Book Is Organized

Like all *For Dummies* books, *Photo Printing & Editing For Dummies* is organized to help you get something done as quickly and painlessly as possible — specifically, to prepare your digital photos for printing or publishing on the Web. This book includes three main parts and a Bonus section, divvied up as follows:

Part I: Take Your Best Shot

Are you photographically challenged? Are your pictures too dark, too light, too blurry, or just plain boring? This part reveals the secret to capturing perfectly exposed, perfectly focused photographs, along with tips for composing more powerful, more exciting images.

Part II: Can I Get a Hard Copy, Please?

After you fill up your camera with photos, you want to get them out into the world, usually as prints. Chapters in this part show you how to do just that, giving you a thorough overview of photo printer and paper options.

Part III: The Part of Tens

A standard feature of all *For Dummies* books, each Part of Tens chapter provides you with ten useful bits of information. Chapter 6 gives you ten ways to turn out better digital photos, while Chapter 7 provides ten ideas for ways to use your digital photos you may not even have thought of yet.

Bonus Section: User Guide

Got a question about using the Digital Photos For Dummies software? Turn to this concise guide for answers. From installing the software on your computer to getting familiar with the software's features, the User Guide presents the explanations and steps you need to work with confidence.

Icons Used in This Book

The little graphic symbols you see dotted throughout this book highlight the following points:

This icon marks stuff you should commit to memory to make your digital photo experiments less stressful.

Text marked with this icon breaks technical gobbledy-gook down into plain English.

This icon points out suggestions that can save you time and energy and perhaps spare you a headache or two.

When you see this icon, pay attention! These tips keep you out of digital trouble and help you find out how to fix things if you leaped before you looked.

Where to Go from Here!

You can read this book from cover to cover, skip around from icon to icon, pick it up and lay it back down while you go get a cup of java. Whatever way you use this book, you're bound to find loads of information that can increase your digital photography skills tenfold. Read a little every day, and you'll discover a whole new way to communicate, whether you're shooting for business, for pleasure, or for both.

Part I
Take Your Best Shot

The 5th Wave   By Rich Tennant

WILDLIFE SAFARI

"Add some interest to the shot by putting the partridge in the foreground."

In this part . . .

Digital cameras for the consumer market are catergorized as "point-and-shoot" cameras. That is, you're supposed to be able to simply point the camera at your subject and shoot the picture. But digital picture-taking isn't quite as automatic as the camera manufacturers would like you to believe. Before you aim that lens and press the shutter button, you need to consider quite a few factors if you want to come away with a good picture, as this part explains.

This part tells you everything you need to know about composition, lighting, and focus — three primary components of a great photograph. It also covers issues specific to digital photography, such as choosing the right capture resolution and avoiding the perils of parallax.

Chapter 1

Keeping Composed and Focused

· ·

In This Chapter

▶ Composing your image for maximum impact

▶ Avoiding viewfinder mistakes

▶ Bringing your subject into focus

· ·

*A*fter you figure out the mechanics of your camera — how to load the batteries, how to turn on the LCD, and so on — taking a picture is a simple process. Just aim the camera and press the shutter button. Taking a *good* picture, however, isn't so easy. Sure, you can record an okay image of your subject without much effort. But if you want a crisp, well-exposed, dynamic image, you need to consider a few factors before you point and shoot.

This chapter explores two basic elements that go into a superior image: composition and focus. See Chapter 2 for detailed info on lighting, which also plays a major role in how your digital photos turn out.

Composition 101

Consider the image in Figure 1-1. As pictures go, it's not bad. The subject, a statue at the base of the Soldiers and Sailors Monument in Indianapolis, is interesting enough. But overall, the picture is . . . well, boring.

Figure 1-1: This image falls flat because of its uninspired framing and angle of view.

Now look at Figure 1-2, which shows two additional images of the same subject, but with more powerful results. What makes the difference? In a word, *composition*. Simply framing the statue differently, zooming in for a closer view, and changing the camera angle create more captivating images.

Figure 1-2: Getting closer to the subject and shooting from less-obvious angles result in more interesting pictures.

Not everyone agrees on the "best" ways to compose an image — art being in the eye of the beholder and all that. For every composition rule, you can find an incredible image that proves the exception. That said, the following list offers some suggestions that can help you create images that rise above the ho-hum mark on the visual interest meter:

✔ Remember the rule of thirds. For maximum impact, don't place your subject smack in the center of the frame, as was done in Figure 1-1. Instead, mentally divide the image area into thirds, as illustrated in Figure 1-3. Then position the main subject elements at spots where the dividing lines intersect.

Figure 1-3: One rule of composition is to divide the frame into thirds and position the main subject at one of the intersection points.

✔ To add life to your images, compose the scene so
   that the viewer's eye is naturally drawn from one
   edge of the frame to the other, as in Figure 1-4. The
   figure in the image appears ready to fly off into the
   big, blue yonder. You can almost feel the breeze
   blowing the torch's flame.

Figure 1-4: To add life to your pictures, frame the scene so
that the eye is naturally drawn from one edge of the image
to the other.

↳ Avoid the plant-on-the-head syndrome. In other words, watch out for distracting background elements such as the flower and computer monitor in Figure 1-5.

↳ Shoot your subject from unexpected angles. Again, refer to Figure 1-1. This image accurately represents the statue. But the picture is hardly as captivating as the images in Figure 1-2, which show the same subject from more unusual angles.

Figure 1-5: This photo provides a classic example of a beautiful subject set against a horrendous background.

✔ Here's a trick for shooting children: Photograph them while they're lying down on the floor and looking up at the camera. Maybe the children you photograph live in pristine surroundings, but in my family, rooms full of children are also full of toys, sippy cups, and other kid paraphernalia, which can make getting an uncluttered shot difficult. So I simply shove everything off to a small area of carpet and have the kids get down on the floor and pose.

✔ Another good approach for shooting the wee ones is to hunker down so that you can shoot at eye level, as I did in Figure 1-6. The results are worth the effort of getting on your knees.

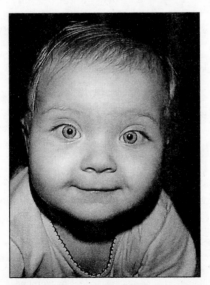

Figure 1-6: Getting down to eye level is another good tactic for shooting kid pics.

✔ Get close to your subject. Often, the most interesting shot is the one that reveals the small details,
such as the laugh lines in a grandfather's face or the
raindrop on the rose petal. Don't be afraid to fill the
frame with your subject, either. The old rule about
"head room" — providing a nice margin of space
above and to the sides of a subject's head — is a
rule meant to be broken on occasion.

✔ Try to capture the subject's personality. The most
boring people shots are those in which the subjects
stand in front of the camera and say "cheese" on the
photographer's cue. If you really want to reveal
something about your subjects, catch them in the
act of enjoying a favorite hobby or using the tools of
their trade. This tactic is especially helpful with subjects who are camera-shy; focusing their attention
on a familiar activity helps put them at ease and
replace that stiff, I'd-rather-be-anywhere-but-here
look with a more natural expression.

A Parallax! A Parallax!

You compose your photo perfectly. The light is fine, the
focus is fine, and all other photographic planets appear
to be in alignment. But after you snap your picture and
view the image on the camera monitor, the framing is off,
as though your subject repositioned itself while you
weren't looking.

You're not the victim of some cruel digital hoax — just a
photographic phenomenon known as a *parallax error.*

On most digital cameras, as on most point-and-shoot film cameras, the viewfinder looks out on the world through a separate window from the camera lens. Because the viewfinder is located an inch or so above or to the side of the lens, it sees your subject from a slightly different angle than the lens. But the image is captured from the point of view of the lens, not the viewfinder.

When you look through your viewfinder, you should see some lines near the corners of the frame. The lines indicate the boundaries of the frame as seen by the camera lens. Pay attention to these framing cues, or you may wind up with pictures that appear to have been lopped off along one edge, as in Figure 1-7.

Figure 1-7: My pal Bernie loses his ears as the result of a parallax error.

The closer you are to your subject, the bigger the parallax problem becomes, whether you use a zoom lens or simply position the camera lens nearer to your subject. Some cameras provide a second set of framing marks in the viewfinder to indicate the framing boundaries that apply when you're shooting close-up shots. Check your camera manual to determine which framing marks mean what. (Some markings have to do with focusing, not framing.)

If your camera has an LCD monitor, you have an additional aid for avoiding parallax problems. Because the monitor reflects the image as seen by the lens, you can simply use the monitor instead of the viewfinder to frame your image. On some cameras, the LCD monitor turns on automatically when you switch to macro mode for close-up shooting.

Focus on Focus

Like point-and-shoot film cameras, digital cameras typically provide focusing aids to help you capture sharp images with ease. The following sections describe the different types of focusing schemes available and explain how to make the most of them.

Working with fixed-focus cameras

Fixed-focus cameras are just that — the focus is set at the factory and can't be changed. The camera is designed to capture sharply any subject within a certain distance from the lens. Subjects outside that range appear blurry.

Fixed-focus cameras sometimes are called *focus-free* cameras because you're free of the chore of setting the focus before you shoot. But even though you can't adjust the focus, you have to remember to keep the subject within the camera's focusing range.

Be sure to check your camera manual to find out how much distance to put between your camera and your subject. With fixed-focus cameras, blurry images usually result from having your subject too close to the camera. (Most fixed-focus cameras are engineered to focus sharply from a few feet away from the camera to infinity.)

Taking advantage of autofocus

Most digital cameras offer autofocus, which means that the camera automatically adjusts the focus after measuring the distance between lens and subject. But "autofocusing" isn't totally automatic. For autofocus to work, you need to "lock in" the focus before you shoot the picture, as follows:

1. **Frame the picture.**

2. **Press the shutter button halfway down and hold it there.**

   Your camera analyzes the picture and sets the focus. If your camera offers autoexposure — as most do — the exposure is set at the same time. After the exposure and focus are locked in, the camera lets you know that you can proceed with the picture. Usually, a little light blinks near the viewfinder, or the camera makes a beeping noise.

3. **Press the shutter button the rest of the way down to take the picture.**

Although autofocus is a great photography tool, you need to understand a few things about how your camera goes about its focusing work in order to take full advantage of this feature. Following is the condensed version of the autofocusing manual.

Autofocus mechanisms fall into one of two main categories:

- ✔ **Single-spot focus:** With this type of autofocus, the camera reads the distance of the element that's at the center of the frame in order to set the focus.

- ✔ **Multi-spot focus:** The camera measures the distance at several spots around the frame and sets focus relative to the nearest object.

You need to know how your camera adjusts focus so that when you lock in the focus (using the press-and-hold method just described), you place the subject within the area that the autofocus mechanism will read. If the camera uses single-spot focusing, for example, you should place your subject in the center of the frame when locking the focus. Some cameras enable you to choose which type of focusing you want to use for a particular shot; check your camera manual for details.

If your camera offers single-spot focus, you may see little framing marks in the viewfinder that indicate the focus point. Check your camera manual to see what the different viewfinder marks mean.

After you lock in the focus, you can reframe your picture if you want. As long as you keep the shutter button halfway down, the focus remains locked. Be careful that the distance between the camera and the subject doesn't change, or your focus will be off.

Focusing manually

On most consumer digital cameras, you get either no manual focusing options or just one or two options in addition to autofocus. You may be able to choose a special focus setting, often called *macro mode,* for close-up shooting and an *infinity lock,* or *landscape mode,* for faraway subjects. When you switch to these modes, make sure that your subject falls within the focusing range of the selected mode. Check your camera's manual to find out the proper camera-to-subject distance.

But a few high-end cameras offer more extensive manual focusing controls. Although some models offer a traditional focusing mechanism where you twist the lens barrel to set the focus, most cameras require you to use menu controls to select the distance at which you want the camera to focus.

The ability to set the focus at a specific distance from the camera comes in handy when you want to shoot several pictures of one, nonmoving subject. By setting the focus manually, you don't have to go to the trouble of locking in the autofocus for each shot. Just be sure that you've accurately gauged the distance between camera and subject when setting the manual-focus distance.

If you're using manual focus for close-up shooting, get out a ruler and make sure that you have the correct camera-to-subject distance. You can't tell whether the focus is dead-on from the viewfinder or LCD, and being just an inch off can mean a blurry picture.

Hold that thing still!

A blurry image isn't always the result of poor focusing; you can also get fuzzy shots if you move the camera during the time the image is being captured.

Holding the camera still is essential in any shooting situation, but it becomes especially important when the light is dim because a longer exposure time is needed. That means that you have to keep the camera steady longer than you do when shooting in bright light.

To help keep the camera still, try these tricks:

🠖 Press your elbows against your sides as you snap the picture.

🠖 Squeeze, don't jab, the shutter button. Use a soft touch to minimize the chance of moving the camera when you press the shutter button.

🠖 Place the camera on a countertop, table, or other still surface. Better yet, use a tripod. You can pick up an inexpensive tripod for about $20.

🠖 If your camera offers a self-timer feature, you can opt for hands-free shooting to eliminate any possibility of camera shake. Place the camera on a tripod (or other still surface), set the camera to self-timer mode, and then press the shutter button (or do whatever your manual says to activate the self-timer mechanism). Then move away from the camera. After a few seconds, the camera snaps the picture for you automatically.

Of course, if you're lucky enough to own a camera that offers remote-control shooting, you can take advantage of that feature instead of the self-timer mode.

Chapter 2

Let There Be Light

● ●

In This Chapter

▶ Shooting with and without a flash

▶ Adjusting exposure

▶ Compensating for backlighting

● ●

Digital cameras are extremely demanding when it comes to light. A typical digital camera has a light sensitivity equivalent to that of ISO 100 film, which is pretty slow. As a result, image detail tends to get lost when objects are in the shadows. Too much light can also create problems. A ray of sunshine bouncing off a highly reflective surface can cause *blown highlights* — areas where all image detail is lost, resulting in a big white blob in your picture.

Capturing just the right amount of light involves not only deciding whether to use a flash, but also figuring out the right exposure settings. The following sections address everything you need to know to capture a well-lit, properly exposed image.

Keep in mind that you can correct minor lighting and exposure problems with the Digital Photos For Dummies software. Generally speaking, making a too-dark image brighter is easier than correcting an overexposed (too bright) image.

Locking in Autoexposure

Exposure refers to the amount of light captured by the camera. Most consumer-level digital cameras feature *autoexposure,* in which the camera reads the amount of light in the scene and then sets the exposure automatically for you.

In order for your camera's autoexposure mechanism to work correctly, take this three-step approach to shooting pictures:

1. **Frame your subject.**

2. **Press the shutter button halfway down and hold it there.**

   The camera analyzes the scene and sets the focus and exposure. (See Chapter 1 on how to work with the autofocus feature.) After the camera makes its decisions, it signals you in some fashion — usually with a blinking light near the viewfinder or with a beeping noise.

   If you don't want your subject to appear in the middle of the frame, you can recompose the image after locking in the exposure and focus. Just keep holding the shutter button halfway down as you reframe the image in your viewfinder. Don't move or reposition the subject before you shoot, or the exposure and focus may be out of whack.

3. Press the shutter button the rest of the way down to take the picture.

On lower-end cameras, you typically get a choice of two autoexposure settings — one appropriate for shooting in very bright light and another for average lighting. Many cameras display a warning light or refuse to capture the image if you've chosen an autoexposure setting that will result in a badly overexposed or underexposed picture. Higher-priced cameras give you more control over auto-exposure, as discussed in the next few sections.

But it looked good in the LCD!

If your camera has an LCD monitor, you can get a good idea of whether your image is properly exposed by reviewing it in the monitor. But don't rely entirely on the monitor, because it doesn't provide an absolutely accurate rendition of your image. Your actual image may be brighter or darker than it appears on the monitor, especially if your camera enables you to adjust the brightness of the monitor display.

To make sure that you get at least one correctly exposed image, *bracket* your shots if your camera offers exposure-adjustment controls. Bracketing means to record the same scene at several different exposure settings. Some cameras even offer an automatic bracketing feature that records multiple images, each at a different exposure, with one press of the shutter button.

Choosing a metering mode

Some higher-priced digital cameras enable you to choose from several *metering modes.* (Check your manual to find out what buttons or menu commands to use to access the different modes.) In plain English, *metering mode* refers to the way in which the camera's autoexposure mechanism meters — measures — the light in the scene while calculating the proper exposure for your photo-graph. The typical options are as follows:

✔ **Matrix metering:** Sometimes known as *multizone metering,* this mode divides the frame into a grid (matrix) and analyzes the light at many different points on the grid. The camera then chooses an exposure that best captures both shadowed and brightly lit portions of the scene. This mode is typically the default setting and works well in most situations.

✔ **Center-weighted metering:** When set to this mode, the camera measures the light in the entire frame but assigns a greater importance — weight — to the center quarter of the frame. Use this mode when you're more concerned about how stuff in the center of your picture looks than stuff around the edges. (How's that for technical advice?)

✔ **Spot metering:** In this mode, the camera measures the light only at the center of the frame. Spot meter-ing is helpful when the background is much brighter than the subject — for example, when you're shoot-ing backlit scenes (subjects that are in front of the sun or another light source).

In matrix or center-weighted metering mode, your subject may be underexposed because the camera reduces the exposure to account for the brightness of the background, as illustrated by the top two examples in Figure 2-1. In the bottom example, I used spot metering mode to properly expose the subject's face.

Figure 2-1: Matrix metering (top left) and center-weighted metering (top right) underexposed the subject due to the bright background light. Spot metering (bottom) exposes the image based on the light on the subject's face.

Adjusting ISO

As you may know if you're used to film cameras, film is assigned an ISO number to indicate light sensitivity. The higher the number, the "faster" the film — meaning that it reacts more quickly to light, enabling you to shoot in dim lighting without a flash or to use a faster shutter speed or smaller aperture.

Some digital cameras also offer a choice of ISO settings, which theoretically gives you the same flexibility as working with different speeds of film. I say "theoretically" because raising the ISO has a downside that usually outweighs the potential advantage.

Pictures shot at a higher ISO tend to suffer from *noise,* which is a fancy way of referring to a speckled, grainy texture. Faster film also produces grainier pictures than slower film, but the quality difference seems to be greater when you shoot digitally. When you print pictures at a small size, the texture produced by the excess grain may not be apparent to the eye; instead, the image may have a slightly blurry look. Often, each shift up in ISO means a step down in image quality.

However, for some shooting scenarios, you may be forced to use a higher ISO if you want to get the picture. If you want to take a picturesque shot at twilight, for example, the camera may not be able to produce a properly exposed photo at all at the lower ISO settings. And if you're trying to capture a moving subject, you may need to raise the ISO in order to use the fast shutter speed necessary to freeze the action.

The bottom line is this: Experiment with ISO settings if your camera offers them, and by all means, go with a higher ISO if the alternative is not getting the shot at all.

But for best picture quality, keep the ISO at its lowest or next-to-lowest setting.

Applying exposure compensation

Different cameras provide you with different ranges of exposure options, and the extent to which an adjustment in exposure affects your image also varies.

Exposure compensation, also referred to as EV *(exposure value)* adjustment, bumps the exposure up or down a few notches from what the camera delivers at the autoexposure setting. How you get to the exposure compensation settings varies from camera to camera. But you typically choose from settings such as +0.7, +0.3, 0.0, –0.3, –0.7, and so on, with the 0.0 representing the default autoexposure setting. A positive EV value increases the exposure, resulting in a brighter image. To decrease the exposure, choose a negative EV value.

Using aperture- or shutter-priority mode

High-end consumer models of digital cameras enable you to switch from regular autoexposure mode, where the camera sets both aperture and shutter speed, to *aperture-priority* autoexposure or *shutter-priority* autoexposure. These options work as follows:

✔ **Aperture-priority autoexposure:** This mode gives you control over the aperture. After setting the aperture, you frame your shot and then press the shutter button halfway down to set the focus and exposure, as you do when using programmed autoexposure mode. But this time, the camera checks to see what aperture you chose and then selects the shutter speed necessary to correctly expose the image at that aperture. By altering the aperture, you can control *depth of field* — the range of sharp focus.

✔ **Shutter-priority autoexposure:** If you work in shutter-priority mode, you choose the shutter speed, and the camera selects the correct aperture.

Switching to shutter-priority or aperture-priority mode can come in handy in the following scenarios:

✔ You can't get the camera to produce the exposure you want in programmed autoexposure mode.

✔ You're trying to capture an action scene, and the shutter speed the camera selects in programmed autoexposure mode is too slow.

✔ You purposefully want to use a too-slow shutter speed so that your picture looks a little blurry, creating a sense of motion.

Adding a Flash of Light

If the techniques discussed in preceding sections don't deliver a bright enough exposure, you simply have to find a way to bring more light onto your subject. The obvious choice, of course, is to use a flash.

Most digital cameras, like point-and-shoot film cameras, have a built-in flash that operates in several modes. You typically can choose from these options:

✔ **Auto flash:** In this mode, which is usually the default setting, the camera gauges the available light and fires the flash if needed.

✔ **Fill flash:** This mode triggers the flash regardless of the light in the scene. Fill-flash mode is especially helpful for outdoor shots, such as the one in Figure 2-2. Because this picture was taken on a bright, sunny day, the camera didn't see the need for a flash in the picture on the left. But turning on the fill-flash mode threw some additional light on the subject's face, bringing her eyes into visible range.

✔ **No flash:** Choose this setting when you don't want to use the flash, no way, no how. With digital photography, you may find yourself using this mode more than you may expect. For example, you may want to turn off the flash because the quality of the existing light, or the interplay of light and shadows, is what makes the scene compelling.

When you turn off the flash, remember that the camera may reduce the shutter speed to compensate for the dim lighting. That means that you need to hold the camera steady to avoid blurry images. Use a tripod or otherwise brace the camera for best results.

Figure 2-2: An outdoor image shot without a flash (left) and with a flash (right).

✔ **Flash with red-eye reduction:** Anyone who's taken people pictures with a point-and-shoot camera is familiar with the so-called red-eye problem. The flash reflects in the subject's eyes, and the result is a demonic red glint in the eye. Red-eye reduction mode aims to thwart this phenomenon by firing a low-power flash before the "real" flash goes off or by lighting a little lamp for a second or two prior to capturing the image. Unfortunately, red-eye reduction on digital cameras doesn't work much better than it does on film cameras.

The good news is that, because you're shooting digitally, you can edit out those red eyes with a simple tool in the Digital Photos For Dummies software.

Switching on additional light sources

Although a flash offers one alternative for lighting your scene, it isn't always the answer. When you're shooting your subject at close range, a flash can cause blown highlights or overexpose some portions of the image.

But you really don't need to go out and spend a fortune on lighting equipment. If you get creative, you can probably figure out a lighting solution using stuff you already have around the house. For example, when shooting small objects, I sometimes clear off a shelf on the white bookcase in my office. A nearby window offers a perfect natural light source. A bright backdrop drape may also provide the contrast you need.

More flashy lighting techniques

A few higher-end cameras offer these variations on the auto-flash mode:

✔ **Slow-sync flash:** With a normal flash, your main subject may be illuminated by the flash, but background elements beyond the reach of the flash may be obscured. With slow-sync flash, a longer exposure time helps make those background elements brighter.

✔ **External flash:** Another high-end option enables you to use a separate flash unit with your digital camera. In this mode, the camera's on-board flash is disabled, and you must set the correct exposure to work with your flash. This option is great for advanced photo hobbyists who have the expertise and equipment to use it.

If your camera has a built-in flash but doesn't offer an accessory off-camera flash connection, you can get the benefits of an external flash by using so-called "slave" flash units. These small, self-contained, battery-operated flash units have built-in photo eyes that trigger the supplemental flash when the camera's flash goes off. If you're trying to photograph an event in a room that's dimly lit, you can put several slave units in different places. All the units will fire when you take a picture anywhere in the room.

When using an artificial light source, whether it is a true-blue photography light or a makeshift solution like a desk lamp, you get better results if you don't aim the light directly at the object you're photographing. Instead, aim the light at the background and let the light bounce off that surface onto your subject.

Compensating for backlighting

A *backlit* picture is one in which the sun or light source is behind the subject. With autoexposure cameras, strong backlighting often results in too-dark subjects because the camera sets the exposure based on the light in the overall scene, not just on the light falling on the subject.

The left image in Figure 2-3 is a classic example of a backlighting problem. To remedy the situation, you have several options:

🗸 Reposition the subject so that the sun is behind the camera instead of behind the subject.

🗸 Reposition yourself so that you're shooting from a different angle.

🗸 Use a flash. Adding the flash can light up your subjects and bring them out of the shadows. However, because the working range of the flash on most consumer digital cameras is relatively small, your subject must be fairly close to the camera for the flash to do any good.

🗸 If the backlighting isn't terribly strong and your camera offers exposure compensation, try raising the EV value, as explained in "Applying exposure compensation," earlier in this chapter.

Keep in mind that while increasing the exposure may brighten up your subjects, the already bright portions of the scene may appear overexposed.

🗸 If your camera offers a choice of metering modes, switch to spot-metering or center-weighted metering. Check out "Choosing a metering mode," earlier in this chapter, for more details.

✔ On cameras that only consider the light throughout the frame when setting the exposure, you can try to "fool" the autoexposure meter. Fill the frame with a dark object, press the shutter button halfway down to lock in the exposure, reframe the subject, and press the shutter button the rest of the way down to take the picture.

Because the focus is also set when you press the shutter button halfway, be sure that the dark object you're using to set the exposure is the same distance from the camera as your real subject. Otherwise, the focus of the picture will be off.

Figure 2-3: Backlighting can cause your subjects to appear lost in the shadows (left). Adjusting the exposure or using a flash can compensate for backlighting (right).

A little bit of additional brightness adjustment with the Digital Photos For Dummies software can also improve things in a backlit image. See the User Guide in the Bonus Section for how to use the brightness tool.

Adding more light to a scene is considerably easier than reducing the light. If you're shooting outdoors, you can't exactly hit the dimmer switch on the sun. If the light is too strong, you really have only a few options. You can move the subject into the shade (in which case you can use a fill flash to light the subject), or, on some cameras, reduce the exposure by lowering the EV value.

Chapter 3

Digicam Dilemmas
(And How to Solve Them)

● ●

In This Chapter

▶ Choosing the right resolution and compression settings

▶ Devoting more pixels to your subject

▶ Working with optical and digital zoom

▶ Capturing action

▶ Avoiding grainy images

● ●

*I*n this chapter, you find out how to tackle some of the challenges that are unique to digital photography. You also discover how to alter your shooting strategy to take advantage of the many new possibilities that are open to you now that you've gone digital.

Dialing Your Capture Settings

Before you press the shutter button or even compose your image, you need to make a few decisions about how you want the camera to capture and store your images. Most digital cameras offer you a choice of image resolution and compression settings, and some cameras also enable you to store the image in one or two different file formats.

The following sections help you come to the right conclusions about your camera's resolution, compression, and file-format options.

Setting the capture resolution

Depending on your camera, you may be able to select from two or more image resolution settings. These settings determine how many horizontal and vertical pixels the image will contain. On some cameras, resolution values are specified in pixels — 640 x 480, for example — with the horizontal pixel count always given first. But on other cameras, the different resolution settings go by such vague names as Basic, Fine, Superfine, and so on.

Your camera manual should spell out exactly how you go about changing the image resolution and how many pixels you get with each setting. You should also find information on how many images you can store per megabyte of camera memory at each setting.

When setting the camera resolution, consider the final output of the image. For Web or on-screen pictures, you can get by with 640 x 480 pixels. But if you want to print your picture, choose the capture setting that comes closest to giving you the output resolution that your printer manual recommends.

Here's a brief summary of resolution matters that matter most:

- ✔ Number of pixels across (or down) ÷ printed image width (or height) = output resolution (ppi).

- ✔ For good-quality prints, you typically need an output resolution of 200 to 300 ppi.

- ✔ For on-screen display, think in terms of pixel dimensions, not output resolution. To use a picture on a Web page, in most cases, 640 x 480 is more than enough.

- ✔ Set your camera to capture a resolution at or above what you need for your final picture output. Remember, you can safely toss away pixels later if you want to lower image resolution, but enlarging a print (adding pixels) can reduce image quality.

Of course, the more pixels, the bigger the picture file and the more memory your image consumes. So if your camera has limited memory and you're shooting at a location where you won't be able to download images, you may want to choose a lower resolution setting so that you can fit more pictures into the available memory. Alternatively, you can select a higher degree of image compression (discussed in the next section) to reduce file size.

On some cameras, capture resolution is lowered automatically when you use certain features. For example, many cameras provide a burst mode that enables you to record a series of images with one press of the shutter button (see "Catching a Moving Target," later in this chapter). When you use this mode, most cameras reduce the capture resolution to 640 x 480 pixels or lower. Cameras that offer a choice of ISO settings also typically limit resolution at the highest settings. (Chapter 2 explains ISO.)

Choosing a compression setting

Your camera probably provides a control for choosing the amount of *compression* that is applied to your images. Basically, compression trims some data out of an image file so that its file size is reduced.

Lossless compression removes only redundant image data so that any change in image quality is virtually undetectable. But because lossless compression often doesn't result in a significant shrinking of file size, most digital cameras use *lossy compression,* which is less discriminating. Lossy compression is great at reducing file size, but you pay the price in reduced image quality. The more compression you apply, the more your image suffers.

Typically, compression settings are given the same vague monikers as resolution settings, such as Good/Better/Best or High/Normal/Basic. Remember that these names refer not to the type or amount of compression being applied, but to the resulting image quality. If you set your camera to the Best setting, for example, the image is less compressed than if you choose the Good setting. Of course, the less you compress the image, the larger its file size, and the fewer images you can fit in the available camera memory.

Because all cameras provide different compression options, you need to consult your manual to find out what the options on your particular model do. Typically, you find a chart in the manual that indicates how many images you can fit into a certain amount of memory at different compression settings. But you need to experiment to find out exactly how each setting affects picture quality. Shoot the same image at several different compression settings to get an idea of how much damage you do to your pictures if you opt for a higher degree of compression.

Mind-boggling resolution stuff

The term *resolution* refers to different measurements, depending on whether you're talking about the camera's captured image or the printed image. Keep the following distinctions in mind:

✔ **Camera resolution:** Digital camera manufacturers use the term resolution to describe the number of pixels in the pictures produced by their cameras. A camera's stated resolution might be 640 x 480 pixels, for example. But those values refer to the pixel dimensions a camera can produce, not the number of pixels per inch in the final image. You determine that when you print the image.

✔ **Printer resolution:** Printer resolution is measured in dots per inch (dpi) rather than pixels per inch (ppi). Most printers use multiple dots to reproduce one image pixel, but the concept is similar: In general, the higher the dpi, the smaller the dots, and the better the printed image. Every printer is geared to handle a specific image resolution, so you need to check your printer manual for the right resolution for your model.

For example, suppose that your camera offers the following resolution options: 640 x 480, 1024 x 768, and 1600 x 1200. Your printer manual tells you that the optimum output resolution for quality prints is 300 ppi. If you capture the image at the lowest resolution, the print size at 300 ppi is around 2 x 1.6 inches; at 1024 x 768, you get a print size of about 3.4 x 2.5 inches; at 1600 x 1200, about 5 x 4. (These are just loose guidelines.)

Selecting a file format

Some cameras enable you to select from a few different file formats — JPEG, TIFF, and so on. Some cameras also provide a proprietary format — that is, a format unique to the camera — along with the more standard formats.

Some file formats result in larger image files than others. For example, some cameras enable you to store images as TIFF files with no compression or as JPEG files with some compression. Although you undoubtedly get better image quality from the TIFF option, the number of pictures you can take before you fill up your available camera memory will be much lower than if you select JPEG.

Shoot the same image using the different file formats available on your camera. Then transfer the pictures to your computer and compare the file size of each image. Now you know what format to use when you want to stuff the maximum number of images in your camera's available memory.

The format you select may affect image quality. So inspect your test images for sharpness. When picture quality is a priority, choose the file format that gives you the best-looking images. Keep in mind, though, that you pay for better picture quality with larger file sizes.

All other things being equal, choose a standard file format, such as JPEG or TIFF, over a camera's proprietary image format. Why? Because most proprietary formats aren't supported by image-editing and image-cataloging programs. So before you can edit or catalog your pictures, you have to take the extra step of converting them to a standard file format using the software that came with your camera.

A few cameras provide you with the option of storing images in the FlashPix file format. However, few image-editing programs can work with FlashPix files. So stay away from this format.

The Digital Photos For Dummies software provides a Conversion button to make it easy to convert photos from one format to another. So, for instance, you may want to take high-quality TIFF pictures, but then when you want to post them on a Web page, you can convert them to the more Web-friendly JPEG format.

Zooming In without Losing Out

Many digital cameras offer zoom lenses that enable you to get a close-up perspective on your subject without going to the bother of actually moving toward the subject.

Some cameras provide an *optical zoom,* which is a true zoom lens, just like the one you may have on your film camera. Other cameras offer a *digital zoom,* which isn't a zoom lens at all but a bit of pixel sleight of hand. The next two sections offer some guidelines for working with both types of zooms.

Shooting with an optical (real) zoom

If your camera has an optical zoom, keep these tips in mind before you trigger that zoom button or switch:

✔ The closer you get to your subject, the greater the chance of a parallax error. Chapter 1 explains this phenomenon fully, but in a nutshell, parallax errors cause the image you see in your viewfinder to be different from what your camera's lens sees and records. To make sure that you wind up with the picture you have in mind, frame your picture using the LCD monitor instead of the viewfinder.

- When you zoom in on a subject, you get less of the background in the frame than if you simply move nearer to the subject.

- Zooming to a telephoto setting also tends to make the background blurrier than if you shoot close to the subject. With a short depth of field — which is what you get when you're zoomed in — elements that are close to the camera are sharply focused, but distant background elements are not. When you zoom to a wide-angle lens setting, you have a greater depth of field, so faraway objects may be as sharply focused as your main subject.

Using a digital zoom

Some cameras provide a *digital zoom* rather than an optical zoom. With digital zoom, the camera enlarges the elements at the center of the frame to create the *appearance* that you've zoomed in.

Say that you want to take a picture of a boat that's bobbing in the middle of a lake. You decide to zoom in on the boat and lose the watery surroundings. The camera crops out the lake pixels and magnifies the boat pixels to fill the frame. The end result is no different than if you had captured both boat and lake, cropped the lake away in your photo software, and then enlarged the remaining boat image.

Given that a digital zoom doesn't provide anything you couldn't achieve in your photo software, why would you want to use it? To wind up with smaller image files, which means that you can fit more images in your camera's memory before you have to download. Because the camera is cropping away the pixels around the edge of the frame, you don't have to store those pixels in memory — just the ones devoted to your main subject. If you know that you don't want those extra pixels, go ahead and use the digital zoom. Otherwise, ignore the feature and do your cropping in your Digital Photos For Dummies software.

Catching a Moving Target

Capturing action with most digital cameras isn't an easy proposition. Digital cameras need plenty of light to produce good images. Unless you're shooting in a very bright setting, the shutter speed required to properly expose the image may be too slow to "stop" action — that is, to record a non-blurry image of a moving target.

A burst of fast shooting

Some cameras offer a rapid-fire option, usually known as *burst mode* or *continuous capture mode,* that enables you to shoot a series of images with one press of the shutter button. The camera takes pictures at timed intervals as long as you keep the shutter button pressed. This feature eliminates some of the lag time between pictures (and comes in handy for ace reporters).

Keep in mind that most cameras can shoot only low- or medium-resolution pictures in burst mode (high-resolution pictures would require a longer storage time). And the flash is typically disabled for this capture mode. More importantly, though, timing the shots so that you catch the height of the action is difficult. If you're interested in recording just one particular moment, you may be better off using a regular shooting mode so that you have better control over when each picture is taken.

Compounding the problem, the camera needs a few seconds to establish the autofocus and autoexposure settings before you shoot, plus a few seconds after you shoot to process and store the image in memory. If you're shooting with a flash, you also must give the flash a few seconds to recycle between pictures.

When you're shooting action shots, use these tricks to do a better job of stopping a moving subject in its tracks:

✔ **Lock in focus and exposure in advance.** Press the shutter button halfway down to initiate the autofocus and autoexposure process (if your camera offers these features) well ahead of the time when you want to capture the image. That way, when the action happens, you don't have to wait for the focus and exposure to be set. See Chapters 1 and 2 for more information about locking in focus and exposure.

✔ **Anticipate the shot.** With just about any camera, there's a slight delay between the time you press the shutter button and the time the camera actually records the image. So the trick to catching action is to press the shutter button just a split second *before* the action occurs.

✔ **Turn on the flash.** Even if it's daylight, turning on the flash sometimes causes the camera to select a higher shutter speed, thereby freezing action better. To make sure that the flash is activated, use the fill-flash mode, discussed in Chapter 2, rather than auto-flash mode. Remember, though, that the flash may need time to recycle between shots. So for taking a series of action shots, you may want to turn the flash off.

✔ **Switch to shutter-priority autoexposure mode (if available).** Then select the highest shutter speed the camera provides and take a test shot. If the picture is too dark, lower the shutter speed a notch and retest. Remember, in shutter-priority mode, the camera reads the light in the scene and then sets the aperture as needed to properly expose the image at the shutter speed you select. So if the lighting isn't great, you may not be able to set the shutter speed high enough to stop action. For more about this issue, see Chapter 2.

✔ **Use a lower capture resolution.** The lower the capture resolution, the smaller the image file, and the less time the camera needs to record the image to memory. That means that you can take a second shot sooner than if you captured a high-resolution image.

✔ **If your camera offers an "instant review" feature that automatically displays a picture on the LCD monitor for a few seconds after you shoot the image, turn off the feature.** When it's on, the camera likely won't let you take another picture during the review period.

✔ **Make sure that your camera batteries are fresh.** Weak batteries can sometimes make your camera behave sluggishly.

✔ **Keep the camera turned on.** Because digital cameras suck up battery juice like nobody's business, the natural tendency is to turn off your camera between shots. But digital cameras take a few seconds to warm up after you turn them on — during which time, whatever it was that you were trying to record may have come and gone. Do turn the LCD monitor off, though, to conserve battery power.

Avoiding Digital Freckles

Are your images coming out of your camera looking a little blotchy or dotted with colored speckles? Do some parts of the image have a jagged appearance? If so, the following remedies can cure your pictures:

✔ **Use a lower compression setting.** Jaggedy or blotchy images are often the result of too much compression. Check your camera manual to find out how to choose a lower compression setting.

✔ **Raise the resolution.** Too few pixels can mean blocky-looking — or *pixelated* — images. The larger you print the photo, the worse the problem becomes.

✔ **Increase the lighting.** Photos shot in very low light often take on a grainy appearance.

✔ **Lower the camera's ISO setting (if possible).** Typically, the higher the ISO, the grainier the image. For more on ISO, check out Chapter 2.

Part II
Can I Get a Hard Copy, Please?

The 5th Wave   By Rich Tennant

@RICHTENNANT

"If I'm not gaining weight, then why does this digital image take up 3MB more memory than a comparable one taken six months ago."

In this part . . .

One major advantage of digital photography is how quickly you can go from camera to final output. In minutes, you can print or electronically distribute your images, while your film-based friends are cooling their heels, waiting for their pictures to be developed at the one-hour photo lab.

This part tells you everything you need to get your pictures out of your camera and into the hands of friends, relatives, clients, or anyone else. In addition to exploring the wide range of printer and paper options for different printing needs, these chapters offer tips on how to get the optimum print size and colors for your prints.

Chapter 4

Understanding Your Printer Options

●●●

In This Chapter

▶ Sorting through the maze of printer options

▶ Making your digital prints last

▶ Comparing features when printer shopping

●●●

*T*aking your digital photos from camera or computer to paper involves several decisions, not the least of which is choosing the right printer for the job. This chapter helps you sort through the various issues involved in printing your pictures. In addition to discussing the pros and cons of different types of printers, I offer tips to help you get the best possible output from any printer.

Printer Primer

For the consumer market, several vendors, including Hewlett-Packard, Epson, Olympus, and Canon, sell printers that are specially designed for printing digital photos at home or in the office. Whereas the first photo printers couldn't deliver the quality you got from a professional imaging lab or even your neighborhood photofinisher, some of the newest models deliver prints that are indistinguishable from the best traditional film prints. With some models, you can even output borderless prints as wide as 13 inches.

Each type of printer offers advantages and disadvantages, and the technology you choose depends on your budget, your printing needs, and your print-quality expectations. To help you make sense of things, the following sections discuss the main categories of consumer and small-office printers.

Inkjet printers

Inkjet printing technology is just one of the options you encounter when you go printer shopping. Inkjet printers work by forcing little drops of ink through nozzles onto the paper. Inkjet printers designed for the home office or small business cost anywhere from $50 to $900. Typically, print quality peaks as you reach the $200 price range, though. Higher-priced inkjets offer speedier printing and extra features, such as the ability to output on wider paper, produce borderless prints, hook up to an office network, or print directly from a camera memory card.

Most inkjet printers enable you to print on plain paper or thicker (and more expensive) photographic stock, either with a glossy or matte finish. That flexibility is great because you can print rough drafts and everyday work on plain paper and save the more costly photographic stock for final prints and important projects.

Inkjets fall into two basic categories:

- ✔ General-purpose models, which are engineered to do a decent job on both text and pictures

- ✔ Photo printers, sometimes referred to as *photocentric* printers, which are geared solely toward printing images

Photocentric printers produce better-quality photographic output than all-purpose printers, but they're typically not well suited to everyday text printing because the print speed is slower than on a general-purpose machine.

That's not to say that you should expect lightning-fast prints from a general-purpose inkjet, though. Even on the fastest inkjet, outputting a color image can take several minutes if you use the highest-quality print settings. And with some printers, you can't perform any other functions on your printer until the print job is complete (see the section "Comparison Shopping," later in this chapter).

In addition, the wet ink can cause the paper to warp slightly, and the ink can smear easily until the print dries. (Remember when you were a kid and painted with watercolors in a coloring book? The effect is similar with inkjets, although not as pronounced.) You can lessen both of these effects by using specially coated inkjet paper (see Chapter 5 for more about paper options).

Despite these flaws, inkjets remain a good, economical solution for many users. Newer inkjet models incorporate refined technology that produces much higher image quality, less color bleeding, and less page warping than early models. Images printed on glossy photo stock from the latest photocentric inkjets rival those from a professional imaging lab.

Laser printers

Laser printers use a technology similar to that used in photocopiers. I doubt that you want to know the details, so let me just say that the process involves a laser beam, which produces electric charges on a drum, which rolls toner — the ink, if you will — onto the paper. Heat is applied to the page to permanently affix the toner to the page (which is why pages come out of a laser printer warm).

Color lasers can produce near-photographic quality images as well as excellent text. They're faster than inkjets, and you don't need to use any special paper (although you get better results if you use a high-grade laser paper).

The downside to color lasers? Price. Although they've become much more affordable over the past two years, color lasers still run $1,000 and up. And these printers tend to be big in stature as well as price — this isn't a machine that you can tuck into small corner of your kitchen.

However, if you have the need for high-volume color output, a color laser printer can make sense. Although you pay more up front than you do for an inkjet, you save money over time because the price of *consumables* (toner or ink, plus paper) is usually lower for laser printing than inkjet printing. Many color lasers also offer networked printing, making them attractive to offices where several people share the same printer.

Dye-sub (thermal dye) printers

Dye-sub (short for *dye-sublimation*) printers transfer images to paper using a plastic film or ribbon that's coated with colored dyes. During the printing process, heating elements move across the film, causing the dye to fuse to the paper. Because they rely on heated dye, they are also known as *thermal dye* printers.

Like the newest photocentric inkjet printers, dye-sub printers deliver very good photo quality. Dye-sub printers manufactured for the consumer market fall within the same price range as quality photocentric inkjets, but they present a few disadvantages that may make them less appropriate for your home or office than an inkjet.

First, most dye-sub printers can output only snapshot-size prints, although a few new models can produce 7.5-x-10-inch prints. More important, you have to use special stock designed to work expressly with dye-sub printers. That means that dye-sub printing isn't appropriate for general-purpose documents; these machines are purely photographic tools.

Thermo-Autochrome printers

A handful of printers use Thermo-Autochrome technology. With these printers, you don't have any ink cartridges, sticks of wax, or ribbons of dye. Instead, the image is created using light-sensitive paper — the technology is similar to that found in fax machines that print on thermal paper.

You can find Thermo-Autochrome printers within the same general price range as consumer dye-sub printers.

But as with dye-sub machines, most consumer Thermo-Autochrome printers can output snapshot-size prints only and can't print on plain paper. More important, examples that I've seen from consumer printers that employ this technology don't match dye-sub or good inkjet output, although I will say that the latest crop of Thermo-Autochrome printers does a much better job than earlier models.

How Long Will They Last?

Another important factor to consider when deciding on a printer is print stability — that is, how long can you expect the prints to last?

All photographs are subject to fading and color shifts over time. Researchers say that a standard film print has a life expectancy of anywhere from 10 to 60 years, depending on the photographic paper, the printing process, and exposure to ultraviolet light and airborne pollutants, such as ozone. Those same criteria affect the stability of photos that you output on your home or office printer.

Unfortunately, the two technologies capable of delivering image quality equal to a traditional photograph — dye-sub and inkjet printing — produce prints that can degrade rapidly, especially when displayed in very bright light. Hang a print in front of a sunny window, and you may notice some fading or a change in colors in as little as a few months.

Manufacturers have been scrambling to address this issue, and several possible solutions have been introduced recently. For example, Epson now offers a high-tech archival inkjet printer that promises a print life expectancy of 100 years or more when special Epson inks and papers are used. Several other vendors also make inks and papers that can be used with inkjet printers and that provide a print life of 25 years or more. You may or may not be able to use these products, depending on your printer. (Note that when you use inks not specifically provided by the printer's manufacturer, you may not get the best print quality and you may void the printer's warranty.) Some dye-sub printers add a special protective coating to prints to help extend print life to about the same life expectancy as a traditional photograph.

Protecting your prints

No matter what the type of print, you can help keep its colors bright and true by adhering to the following storage and display guidelines:

✔ If you're having the picture framed, always mount the photo behind a matte to prevent the print from touching the glass. Be sure to use acid-free, archival matte board and UV-protective glass.

✔ Display the picture in a location where it isn't exposed to strong sunlight or fluorescent light for long periods of time.

✔ In photo albums, slip pictures inside acid-free, archival sleeves.

✔ Don't adhere prints to a matte board or other surface using masking tape, scotch tape, or other household products. Instead, use acid-free mounting materials, sold in art-supply stores and some craft stores.

✔ Limit exposure to humidity, wide temperature swings, cigarette smoke, and other airborne pollutants because these can also contribute to image degradation.

✔ For the ultimate protection, always keep a copy of the image file on a CD-ROM or other storage medium so that you can output a new print if the original one deteriorates.

The truth is, though, that no one really knows just how long a print from any of these new printers will last because they just haven't been around that long. The estimates given by manufacturers are based on lab tests that try to simulate the effect of years of exposure to light and atmospheric contaminants. But the research results are pretty varied, and the photo life you can expect from any printing system depends on whose numbers you use.

So Which Printer Should You Buy?

The answer to that question depends on your printing needs and your printing budget. Here are some things to bear in mind on which of the printing technologies works best for which situation:

- If you want the closest thing to traditional photo-graphic prints, go for one of the new photocentric inkjets or dye-sub models. If you go dye-sub, though, remember that you can't print on plain paper.

- If you're buying a printer for use in an office and you want a machine that can handle high-volume print-ing, look into color lasers.

- For home or small-office printing of both text and photos, opt for a general-purpose inkjet model. You can produce good-looking color and grayscale images, although you need to use high-grade paper and the printer's highest quality settings to get the best results. You can print on glossy photographic paper as well.

A brief warning about general-purpose inkjets: Some of the inkjets I've tried have been so slow and had such page-warping problems that I would never consider using them on a daily basis. Others do a really good job, delivering sharp, clean images in a reasonable amount of time, with little evidence of the problems normally associated with this printing technology. The point is, all inkjets are not created equal, so shop carefully.

✔ Multipurpose printers — those that combine a color printer, fax machine, and scanner in one machine — usually don't produce the kind of output that will satisfy most photo enthusiasts. Typically, you sacrifice print quality and/or speed in exchange for the convenience of the all-in-one design. However, a few can deliver good photographic prints.

Keep in mind that most photocentric printers aren't engineered with text printing as the primary goal, so your text may not look as sharp as it would on a low-cost black-and-white laser or inkjet printer. Also, your text printing costs may be higher than on a black-and-white printer because of ink costs.

Comparison Shopping

After you determine which type of printer is best for your needs, you can get down to the nitty-gritty and compare models and brands. Print quality and other features can vary widely from model to model, so do plenty of research.

The easiest feature to compare is the size of print that the machine can produce. You have three basic options:

✔ Standard printers can print on letter-size paper as large as 8.5 x 11 inches. However, most printers can't print all the way to the edge of the paper — in other words, they can't produce borderless photo prints.

✔ Wide-format printers can handle larger paper. The maximum size print you can output varies from model to model. In addition, some wide-format printers can print borderless prints.

✔ Snapshot printers are limited to printing pictures at sizes of 4 x 6 inches or smaller. Most new snapshot printers, can print directly from camera memory cards; however, picture-editing options are limited.

After you get past print size, sorting through the remaining printer features can get a little murky. So here's a translation of the most critical printer data to study when you're shopping:

✔ **Dpi:** Dpi stands for *dots per inch* and refers to the number of dots of color the printer can create per linear inch. You can find consumer-level color printers with resolutions from 300 dpi up to 2800 dpi.

In theory, a higher dpi should mean better-looking images. But because different types of printers create images differently, an image output at 300 dpi on one printer may look considerably better than an image output at the same or even higher dpi on another printer. So although printer manufacturers make a big deal about their printers' resolutions, dpi isn't always a reliable measure of print quality.

✔ **Quality options:** Many printers give you the option of printing at several different quality settings. You can choose a lower quality for printing rough drafts of your images and then bump up the quality for final output. Typically, the higher the quality setting, the longer the print time and, on inkjet printers, the more ink required.

Ask to see a sample image printed at each of the printer's quality settings and determine whether those settings will work for your needs. For example, is the draft quality so poor that you would need to use the highest quality setting even for printing proofs? If so, you may want to choose another printer if you print a lot of drafts.

✔ **Inkjet colors:** Most inkjets print using four colors: cyan, magenta, yellow, and black. This ink combination is known as CMYK (see the sidebar "Leaving CMYK to the pros," later in this chapter). Some lower-end inkjets eliminate the black ink and just combine cyan, magenta, and yellow to approximate black. "Approximate" is the key word — you don't get good, solid blacks without that black ink, so for best color quality, avoid three-color printers.

Some new photocentric inkjets feature six or seven ink colors, adding a light cyan, light magenta, or light black to the standard CMYK mix. The extra inks expand the range of colors that the printer can manufacture, resulting in more accurate color rendition, but add to the print cost.

✔ **Print speed:** If you use your printer for business purposes and you print a lot of images, be sure that the printer you pick can output images at a decent speed. And be sure to find out the per-page print speed for printing at the printer's *highest* quality setting. Most manufacturers list print speeds for the lowest-quality or draft-mode printing.

✔ **Cost per print:** To understand the true cost of a printer, you need to think about how much you'll pay for consumables each time you print a picture. The paper part is easy: Just find out what kind of paper the manufacturer recommends and then go to any computer store or office-supply outlet and check prices for that paper. But you also need to add the cost of ink, toner, or dye to the paper cost.

Manufacturers usually include this data in their brochures or on their Web sites. You usually see costs stated in terms of *x* percentage of coverage per page — for example, "three cents per page at 15 percent coverage." In other words, if your image covers 15 percent of an 8.5 x 11-inch sheet of paper, you spend three cents on toner, ink, or dye.

The problem is that no single standard for calculating this data exists, so you really can't compare apples to apples. One manufacturer may specify per-print costs based on one size image and one print-quality setting, while another uses an entirely different print scenario. As they say in the car ads, your actual mileage may vary.

That said, if you're buying an inkjet printer, you *can* lower your ink costs somewhat by choosing a printer that uses a separate ink cartridge for each ink color (typically, cyan, magenta, yellow, and black) or at least uses a separate cartridge for the black ink. On models that have just one cartridge for all inks, you usually end up throwing away some ink because one color will be depleted before the others.

Also remember that some printers require special cartridges for printing in photographic-quality mode. In some cases, these cartridges lay down a clear overcoat over the printed image. The overcoat gives the image a glossy appearance when printed on plain paper and also helps protect the ink from smearing and fading. In other cases, you put in a cartridge that enables you to print with more colors than usual — for example, if the printer usually prints using four inks, you may insert a special photo cartridge that enables you to print using six inks. These special photographic inks and overlay cartridges are normally more expensive than standard inks. So when you compare output from different printers, find out whether the images were printed with the standard ink setup or with more expensive photographic inks.

✔ **Host-based printing:** With a *host-based printer,* all the data computation necessary to turn pixels into prints is done on your computer, not on the printer. In some cases, the process can tie up your computer entirely — you can't do anything else until the image is finished printing.

If you print relatively few images during the course of a day or week, having your computer unavailable for a few minutes each time you print an image may not be a bother. And host-based printers are generally cheaper than those that do the image processing themselves. But if you print images on a daily basis, you may be frustrated by a printer that ties up your system in this fashion.

On the other hand, if you buy a printer that does its own image processing, be sure that the standard memory that ships with the printer is adequate to print large images at the printer's highest resolution.

✔ **Computer-free printing:** Several manufacturers offer printers that can print directly from your camera or memory cards — no computer required. You insert your memory card, use the printer's control panel to set up the print job, and press the Print button.

Of course, direct printing takes away your chance to edit your pictures; you may be able to use camera or printer settings to make minor changes, such as rotating the image or making the picture brighter, but that's all.

✔ **PostScript printing:** If you want to be able to print graphics created in illustration programs such as Adobe Illustrator and saved in the EPS (Encapsulated PostScript) file format, you need a printer that offers PostScript printing functions.

Although the preceding specifications give you a better idea of which printers do what, be sure to also go to the library and search through computer and photography magazines for reviews of any printer you're considering. In addition, you can get customer feedback on different models by logging onto one of the digital photography or printing newsgroups on the Internet.

Just as with any other major purchase, you should also investigate the printer's warranty — one year is typical, but some printers offer longer warranties. And be sure to find out whether the retail or mail-order company selling the printer charges a *restocking fee* (as much as 15 percent of the purchase price) if you return the printer.

But no matter how many reviews you read or how many questions you ask, you simply can't tell for certain that a particular printer can do the job you need it to do without

Leaving CMYK to the pros

On-screen images are *RGB images,* created by combining red, green, and blue light. Most professional printing presses and most consumer printers create images by mixing four colors of ink — cyan, magenta, yellow, and black. Pictures created using these four colors are called *CMYK images.* If you take your digital images to a service for printing, the printer can convert your images to the CMYK color mode.

Don't convert your images to CMYK for printing on your own printer, because consumer printers are engineered to work with RGB image data. And no matter whether you're printing your own images or having them commercially reproduced, remember that CMYK has a smaller *gamut* than RGB, which is a fancy way of saying that you can't reproduce with inks all the colors you can create with RGB. CMYK can't handle the really vibrant, neon colors you see on your computer monitor, for example, which is why images tend to look a little duller after conversion to CMYK and why your printed images don't always match your on-screen images.

taking the printer home and testing it with your computer and with your own images.

Few stores have printers hooked up to computers, so you can't test-print your own images in the store. Some printers can output samples using the manufacturer's own images, but those images are carefully designed to show the printer at its best and mask any problem areas. So either find a store where you can do your own pre-purchase testing, or make sure that you're not going to pay a hefty fee for the privilege of returning the printer.

After you purchase your printer, don't ignore your printer manual's instructions regarding routine printer maintenance. Print heads can become dirty, inkjet nozzles can become clogged, and all sorts of other gremlins can gunk up the works. When testing an inkjet model for this book, for example, I almost wrote the printer off as a piece of junk because I was getting horrendous printouts. Then I followed the troubleshooting advice in the manual and cleaned the print heads. The difference was like night and day. Suddenly, I was getting beautiful, rich images, just like the printer's advertisements promised.

Chapter 5

Creating Your Own Prints

● ●

In This Chapter
▶ Choosing the right paper for the job
▶ Setting the output size and resolution before printing

● ●

*W*ith paper, as with most things in life, you get what you pay for. The more you're willing to pay for your paper, the more your images will look like traditional print photographs. In fact, if you want to upgrade the quality of your images, simply changing the paper stock can do wonders.

Thumbing through Paper Options

Table 5-1 shows some sample prices of commonly used paper stocks, with the least expensive stocks listed first. If your printer can accept different stocks, print drafts of your images on the cheaper stocks, and reserve the stocks at the end of the table for final output. Note that prices in the table reflect what you can expect to pay in discount office supply or computer stores for 8.5-x-11-inch stock. You can buy photographic stock in other sizes, however, to use with some printers.

Table 5-1	**Paper Types and Costs**	
Type	*Description*	*Cost per Sheet*
Multipurpose	Lightweight, cheap paper designed for everyday use in printers, copiers, and fax machines. Similar to the stuff you've been putting in your photocopier and typewriter for years.	$.01 to .02
Inkjet	Designed specifically to accept inkjet inks. Paper is heavier and treated with special coating that enables ink to dry more quickly, reducing ink smearing, color bleeding, and page curl.	$.01 to .10
Laser	Engineered to work with the toners used in laser printers. "Premium" laser papers are heavier, brighter, and smoother so that images appear sharper.	$.01 to .04
Photo	Thicker stock expressly designed for printing digital photos; creates closest cousin to traditional film print. Available with glossy or matte finish and artistic textures.	$.50 to $2
Dye-sub	Glossy paper specially treated for use with dye-sub printers only.	$1 to $2

Sending Your Image to the Printer

Getting the picture on paper involves only a few steps, because Digital Photos For Dummies makes it simple. Here's the drill:

1. **Select the photos that you want to print in the Digital Photos For Dummies software.** You can do so in either the Explorer window or the Album window.

2. **Click the appropriate Print button.** You can choose either the Print button in the topmost toolbar (if you chose images in the Explorer window) or the Print button in the Album located to the left of the Slideshow button (if you chose images from an album).

   The Print Wizard dialog box appears.

3. **Choose the layout you want.** You can choose from the following:

   Multi-photo sheet: Use this if you want to create multiple smaller photos on each sheet of paper. You can choose from a number of different sizes to print to including wallet size, 5×7, and 4×6.

   Single-photo sheet: This prints a single photo on each sheet of paper.

   Contact sheet: This prints thumbnails of photos that you select from an album or directory. Contact sheets are especially useful for created a quick-reference of your albums.

4. **Specify the quality, orientation, and paper format that you prefer.**

   Always choose draft quality and regular paper the first time you print anything as an inexpensive test. After you are satisfied with the results of your test print, you can switch to glossy paper and higher quality.

5. **Click Next.** The Layout sheet and preview that you see have different options depending on the type of layout that you chose in the previous step.

   The options for Contact sheet and Multi-photo sheet are easy to understand (and you can see the effects immediately in the Preview window), but the options for Single-photo sheet need a bit of explanation. They are as follows:

   Photo Size: You can choose a specific size or Printable area, which uses as much of the printable area as possible.

   You may not be happy with the results you achieve by trying to expand a small image to fill an entire page. Be sure to preview the image before printing and print in draft mode before outputting for higher quality.

   Fitting: Your options are Do not scale images, Scale to fit, and Scale and crop to fit. Most of the time, you want to scale the images, but you should test print before printing to expensive paper, because scaling can cause blurriness.

   Rotate pictures to maximize print surface: This setting allows the program to decide the best printing orientation for you.

6. **After you are satisfied with the Preview, click Finish.** The image is sent to the printer.

See the User Guide in the Bonus Section for more details about printing with the Digital Photos For Dummies software.

Adjusting print size

Because print size affects output resolution and has a major impact on print quality, you need to take care when resizing images prior to printing.

When you enlarge an image, one of two things happens: The resolution goes down and the pixel size increases, or the image-editing software has to add pixels to fill the enlarged area. Both options can result in loss of image quality. Similarly, when you reduce the dimensions of a print, you can retain the current pixel count (so that resolution goes up and pixel size shrinks), or you can retain the current resolution and let the image-editing software dump excess pixels. Because both approaches can harm your image quality, avoid reducing an image by more than 25 percent.

Fortunately, the Resize tool in Digital Photos For Dummies simplifies the resizing process and helps you avoid accidentally distorting your images in the process. You can resize a single image, but it's most convenient for resizing a whole batch of images at once, as you may want to do when you've taken a number of photos at various sizes and want to print them all at the same size. See the User Guide in the Bonus Section for details on resizing.

These colors don't match!

You may notice a significant color shift between your on-screen and printed images. This color shift is because of the inherent difference between creating colors with light and reproducing them with ink (a problem briefly explained in Chapter 4). In addition, the brightness of the paper and the purity of the ink can lead to colors that look different on paper than on-screen.

Although perfect color matching is impossible, you can take a few steps to bring your printer and monitor colors closer together, as follows:

- ✓ Changing your paper stock sometimes affects color rendition. Typically, the better the paper, the truer the color matching.

- ✓ The software provided with most color printers includes color-matching controls that are designed to get your screen and image colors to jibe. Check your printer manual for information on how to access these controls.

- ✓ Don't convert your images to the CMYK color model for printing on a consumer printer. These printers are designed to work with RGB images, so you get better color matching if you work in the RGB mode. (See Chapter 4 for definitions of CMYK and RGB colors.)

- ✓ If your image looks great on-screen but prints too dark, your printer software may offer brightness/ contrast controls that enable you to temporarily lighten the image. You can get better results, though, if you do the job using one of the Digital Photos For Dummies enhancement tools: Auto Levels, Auto Contrast, or Brightness/Contrast. In any case, if you want to make permanent changes to brightness levels, you need to use your image editor, not your printer software. See the User Guide in the Bonus Section for details.

- ✓ Finally, remember that the colors you see both on-screen and on paper vary depending on the light in which you view them.

Part III
The Part of Tens

"I know I don't need a flash in this light, but it stuns them into inactivity long enough for me to compose subsequent shots."

In this part . . .

In the spirit of instant gratification, this part of the book is designed for those folks who want information right away. These chapters present useful tips and ideas in small snippets that you can rush in and snag in seconds. Chapter 6 offers ten techniques for creating better digital images, while Chapter 7 gives you ten creative ideas for ways to do more with your digital photos than simply admiring them in rotation on your screensaver. Hadn't thought of that one, eh? Read on.

Chapter 6

Ten Ways to Improve Your Digital Images

● ●

In This Chapter

▶ Capturing the best digital image you can

▶ Saving photos with optimum compression settings

▶ Correcting flaws with your photo software

▶ Choosing paper for the best prints

● ●

Digital cameras have a high "wow" factor. That is, if you walk into a room full of people and start snapping pictures with your digital camera, just about everyone in the room will say, "Wow!" and ask for a closer look.

Sooner or later, though, people stop being wow-ed by the whiz-bang technology of a digital camera and start taking a closer look at the quality of your photos. So that you don't embarrass yourself — photographically speaking, anyway — this chapter presents ten ways to ensure better digital images. If you pay attention to these guidelines, your audience will be as captivated by your pictures as they are by your nifty camera.

Remember the Resolution!

When you print digital photos, the image output resolution — the number of pixels per linear inch — makes a big impact on picture quality. To get the best results from most printers, you need an output resolution of between 200 to 300 pixels per inch (ppi).

Most digital cameras offer a few different capture settings, each of which delivers a certain number of pixels. Before you take a picture, consider how large you may want to print the photo. Then select the capture setting that gives you the number of pixels you need to be able to print a good picture at that size.

Remember that you usually can get rid of excess pixels in your photo software without affecting picture quality, but you almost never get good results from adding pixels.

Don't Overcompress Your Images

Most cameras enable you to select from several *compression* settings. Compression is a technique used to shrink the size of an image file. In most cases, camera compression settings have quality-related names — Best, Better, Good, for example — because compression affects picture quality.

For the best-looking images, shoot your pictures using the setting that applies the least amount of compression. Of course, less compression means larger file sizes, so you can't fit as many pictures in the camera's memory as you can at a lower-quality setting.

You also need to consider the compression factor when saving your images after editing them. Some file formats, such as JPEG, compress more than others, such as TIFF. See Chapter 3 for details.

Look for the Unexpected Angle

As explored in Chapter 1, changing the angle from which you photograph your subject can add impact and interest to the picture. Instead of shooting a subject straight on, investigate the unexpected angle.

As you compose your scenes, also remember the rule of thirds — divide the frame into vertical and horizontal thirds and position the main focal point of the shot at a spot where the dividing lines intersect.

Light 'Er Up!

Good lighting is essential for good digital pictures. The light sensitivity of most digital cameras is equivalent to the sensitivity of ISO 100 film, which means that shooting in low lighting usually results in dark and grainy images.

If your camera has a flash, you may need to use the flash not just when shooting in dimly lit interiors, but also to bring your subjects out of the shadows when shooting outdoors. See Chapter 2 for more on flashes.

Use a Tripod

To capture the sharpest possible image, you must hold the camera absolutely still. Even the slightest movement can result in a blurry image. Remember that the exposure time required by the average digital camera is compara- ble to that required by ISO 100 film, so you need to hold your digital camera still for a bit longer than when taking a film picture. For best results, use a tripod.

Compose from a Digital Perspective

When you compose pictures, fill as much of the frame as possible with your subject. Try not to waste precious pixels on a background that will be cropped away in the editing process. See Chapter 1 for more composition tips.

Take Advantage of Image-Correction Tools

Don't automatically toss photos that don't look as good as you would like. With some judicious use of the retouching tools in the Digital Photos For Dummies software, you can brighten up under-exposed images, improve color saturation, crop off distracting background elements, and even fix red-eye effects. See the User Guide in the Bonus Section to find out how.

Being able to edit your photographs is one of the major advantages of shooting with a digital camera. After you start using these simple enhancement tools, you'll wonder how you got along without them.

Print Your Images on Good Paper

As discussed in Chapter 4, the type of paper you use when printing your images can have a dramatic effect on how your pictures look. The same picture that looks blurry, dark, and oversaturated when printed on cheap copy paper can look sharp, bright, and glorious when printed on special glossy photographic paper.

Check your printer's manual for information on the ideal paper to use with your model. Some printers are engineered to work with a specific brand of paper, but as new papers are developed, you may find something that works even better than the recommended paper.

Practice, Practice, Practice!

Unlike film photography, where you have to pay for your mistakes by developing the images to see what worked, digital photography enables you to experiment for free. So shoot as many pictures as you can, in as many different light situations as you can. As you shoot, jot down the camera settings you used and the lighting conditions at the time you snapped the image. Later, evaluate the pictures to see which settings worked the best in which situations. In time, you'll develop an instinctive feel for the best techniques for certain scenarios.

Don't share your bad photos. If you take 20 shots and only 10 turn out well, show off those top 10 and delete the rest. Your reputation as a good photographer will soar.

Read the Manual (Gasp!)

Remember that instruction manual that came with your camera? The one you promptly stuffed in a drawer without bothering to read? Go get it. Then sit down and spend an hour devouring every bit of information inside it.

I know, I know. Manuals are deadly boring, which is why you invested in this software and entertaining little book. But you won't get the best pictures out of your camera unless you understand how all its controls work. This book can give you general recommendations and instructions, but for camera-specific information, the best resource is the manufacturer's own manual.

Chapter 7

Ten Great Uses for Digital Images

- -

In This Chapter

▶ Sharing pictures with others on the Web or via e-mail

▶ Creating and posting digital photo albums

▶ Publishing custom calendars, greeting cards, or stationery

▶ Adding pictures to business and marketing documents

▶ Printing and framing your best work

- -

This chapter enables you to enjoy the long version of my enthusiastic "what you can do with digital photos" speech in the safety of your own home or office. Feel free to leave at any time for coffee — I'll be here with more ideas when you come back.

Design a More Exciting Web Site

Perhaps the most popular use for digital images is to spice up World Wide Web sites. You can include pictures of your company's product, headquarters, or staff on your Web site to help potential customers get a better idea of who you are and what you're selling.

You can also create a personal Web page for yourself or your family. Many Internet service providers make a limited amount of free space available for those who want to publish personal Web pages. And with today's Web-page creation software, the process of designing, creating, and maintaining a Web page isn't all that difficult. Check out *Creating Web Pages For Dummies,* 6th Edition (Wiley Publishing, Inc.).

E-Mail Pictures to Friends and Family

By attaching a photo to an e-mail message, you can share pictures with friends, family, and colleagues around the world in a matter of minutes. No more waiting for the film lab to develop and print your pictures (or extra reprints). Just snap the picture, download it to your computer, and click the Send button in your e-mail program.

Create Online Photo Albums

If you regularly have batches of pictures that you want to share, check out online photo-sharing sites. You can create personal digital photo albums with the Digital Photos For Dummies software and then invite other people to visit the site to view — or even print — your pictures.

Creating and maintaining an online album is easy, thanks to user-friendly tools available at each site. Best of all, posting and sharing albums is usually free. You pay only for prints that you order.

To get started, check out these leading photo-sharing sites:

- ✔ www.ofoto.com
- ✔ www.shutterfly.com
- ✔ www.nikonnet.com
- ✔ www.fujifilm.net

One word of caution: Don't rely on a photo-sharing site for storage of important, irreplaceable photos. If the site experiences problems, your photos could be lost. Always keep copies of your pictures on your own computer or removable storage media.

Add Impact to Sales Materials

Using a desktop publishing program such as Adobe PageMaker or Microsoft Publisher, you can easily add your digital photos to brochures, fliers, newsletters, and other marketing materials. You can also use your images in multimedia presentations created in Microsoft PowerPoint or Corel Presentations.

For best results, size your pictures to the desired dimensions and resolution in your Digital Photos For Dummies software before you place them into your presentation or publishing program.

Make an Old-Fashioned Scrapbook

A scrapbook is a creative way to preserve your printed digital photos and use up paper scraps and stickers (or invest in more artistic ornamental scraps). You can use the scrapbook templates in the Digital Photos For Dummies software to print your photos in fun and fancy shapes to liven up the look of each page, or you can find special scissors at craft stores to cut out your printed pics with wavy edges. Add silly or sentimental memories in your own handwriting or in a font that matches your scrapbook theme, and you have a keepsake to present or treasure for years to come.

If you really want your scrapbook to last unto the next generation, work only with special acid-free scrapbooking materials available in craft and photo shops and use high-quality paper for printing your digital photos, as explained in Chapter 4.

Print Photo Calendars and Cards

You can use an ordinary word-processing program or special software to create customized calendars featuring your images. The only decision you need to make is which picture to put on December's page and which one to use on July's. You can also scope out Greeting Cards For Dummies software for designing personalized greeting cards and stationery.

Don't forget that the paper you use to print your stationery or cards plays a large role in how professional the finished product appears. If you're printing the piece yourself, invest in some high-quality paper or special greeting-card stock, available as an accessory for many color printers.

Include Digipics in Databases

You can add digital images to company databases and spreadsheets in order to provide employees with visual as well as text information. For example, if you work in human resources, you can insert employee pictures into your employee database. Or if you're a small-business owner and maintain a product inventory in a spreadsheet program, you can insert pictures of individual products to help you remember which items go with which order numbers.

Put a Name with the Face

You can put digital pictures on business cards, employee badges, and nametags for guests at a conference or other large gathering. I love getting business cards that include the person's face, for example, because I'm one of those people who never forgets a face but almost always has trouble remembering the name.

Exchange a Picture for a Thousand Words

Don't forget the power of a photograph to convey an idea or describe a scene. Did your roof suffer damage in a windstorm? Take pictures of the damage and e-mail them to your insurance agent and roofing contractor. Looking for a bookcase to fit in with your existing office decor? Take a picture of your office to the furniture store and ask for suggestions.

Hang a Masterpiece on Your Wall

Naturally, you can always simply print and frame your favorite images.

For the best-looking pictures, print your image on a dye-sub printer or photo inkjet using top-grade photo paper. If you don't own such a printer, you can take the image file to a commercial printer or photo-finishing lab for output.

Keep in mind that prints from dye-sub and inkjet printers do fade when exposed to sunlight, so for those really important pictures, you may want to invest in a frame that has UV-protective glass. Also, hang your picture in a spot where it won't get pummeled with strong light on a regular basis, and be sure to keep a copy of the original image file so that you can reprint the image if it fades too badly.

Bonus Section

User Guide

● ●

In This Section

▶ Getting up and running

▶ Loading up images from your digital camera

▶ Using albums to organize and view your photos

▶ Enhancing your images

▶ Printing your photos

● ●

*D*igital photography's popularity continues to grow, and who knows where it may end? In light of the sheer number of cameras sold over the last couple of years, Digital Photos For Dummies seeks to provide everyone using these new technologies with a photo editing program that is both easy to use and guarantees results.

Thanks to its ergonomic design and intuitive interface, using the Digital Photos For Dummies software is a snap for both beginners and digital photo enthusiasts who want quick results. However, before you jump in with both feet, take time out to leaf through this guide to avoid getting lost in the program details and experiencing subsequent fits of frustration. You'll quickly come to realize two things: You don't have to be an expert to retouch your photos, and the only thing holding you back in the world of digital editing is your imagination.

Digital Photos For Dummies enables you to:

 ✔ Acquire your images from your digital camera.

 ✔ Retouch and correct countless flaws.

 ✔ Categorize and easily locate your images.

 ✔ Add special effects.

 ✔ Make up multimedia presentations using your photos.

Installation Instructions

Installing the software from the CD takes just minutes. After you install the Digital Photos For Dummies software on your computer, you can run the program from the Start menu by navigating through the Programs menu to the Anuman Interactive menu. Or, you can just double-click the desktop shortcut. However, be sure to keep the CD in a handy place in case you need to install the software again sometime.

Minimum configuration

You need the following minimum requirements on your computer to use the Digital Photos For Dummies software.

✔ Pentium 100 MHz or higher

✔ Microsoft Windows 98, 2000, Me, XP

✔ 32 MB RAM available

✔ 20 MB free hard disk space

✔ Windows-compatible mouse

✔ Windows-compatible printer

✔ CD-ROM or DVD-ROM drive

Installing the software

Installing the software from the CD takes just minutes. After you install the Home Budget For Dummies software on your computer, you can run the program from the Start menu by navigating through the Programs menu to the Anuman Interactive menu. Or, you can just double-click the desktop shortcut. However, be sure to keep the CD in a handy place in case you need to install the software again sometime.

To install the Digital Photos For Dummies software, follow these steps:

1. **Insert the original Digital Photos For Dummies CD-ROM with the shiny side down into your CD-ROM drive and then close the drive.**

   The installation program begins after a moment. If installation does not launch automatically, complete the set of steps below this one.

2. **Follow the step-by-step instructions that appear on-screen.**

If, for some reason, the installation doesn't begin automatically, just follow these steps:

1. **Click the Start button (located in the lower-left corner of your Windows desktop).**

2. **Click Run.**

3. **Type the command** D:Dummies **in the window that appears.**

   If this command doesn't work, replace the letter D with the letter associated with your CD-ROM drive (E, F, and so on).

4. **Click OK to display the Welcome screen.**

5. **Click Install to begin installing the software on your computer.**

In the Choose Components screen, you can select the components that you want to install. By default, the Documentation and the Shell Extension are selected, and these options are correct for most people. Click Next to continue.

Next, you specify the directory in which you want to store the program. If necessary, indicate a different path from the one selected by default by clicking the Browse button. Then click Next.

In the File Associations screen, you can choose file types to associate with the Digital Photos For Dummies software. Each line corresponds to an image type (JPG, TIF, BMP, PNG or GIF). After selecting a file type, double-clicking on any file of that type will open the picture in Digital Photos For Dummies.

The actual installation process now begins. It takes less than one minute on average, and you can keep track of its progress.

That's it — the software is installed. In this final dialog box, you can choose to create an icon on your desktop and an icon in your Quick Launch bar, which you can then use to run Digital Photos For Dummies.

Customer service

Should you encounter any difficulties in loading or using any of the software, Anuman Interactive offers a comprehensive technical support service:

- ✔ **E-mail** (hotline.us@anuman-interactive.com): E-mail us with your problem, together with as much information as you can supply to aid a speedy response.
- ✔ **Web site** (www.anuman-interactive.com): Visit our Website to find information about all our software.

 If this introductory User Guide does not address all of your questions about the software, please consult the detailed Help files included in the software when you click the ? button.

Getting Started

Digital Photos For Dummies is a simple yet powerful digital photography program. It contains a main window consisting of different menus, buttons, and explorer tools. When you first launch the program, you see the interface, as shown in Figure B-1. The screen may seem a bit cluttered, but you'll soon see that its excellent ergonomic design enables the functions to be picked up and used by almost anyone in no time at all.

Explorer navigation area

Toolbar

Menu bar

Explorer preview area

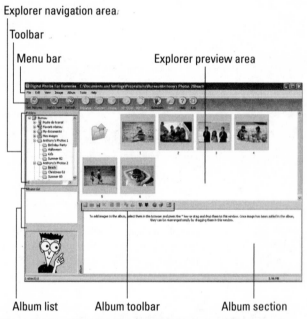

Album list   Album toolbar   Album section

Figure B-1: The Digital Photos For Dummies main window.

The screen that welcomes you when you first launch the software comprises four separate sections; here's a rundown from top to bottom:

- ✔ **Menu bar:** Contains all the functions divided into seven different menus.

- ✔ **Toolbar:** Contains 12 buttons that are either active or inactive, depending on what windows are open and the elements selected.

- ✔ **Explorer:** Takes up the largest part of your workspace and allows you to navigate to the different folders on your hard disk or any other storage device (CD-ROM drive, and so on) and preview images.

- ✔ **Albums List:** Once you create and save albums, you can click any album here and it will open in the Album section.

- ✔ **Album section:** Located at the bottom of the screen, this area enables you to drag and drop images into albums. The album section has its own view window where you can see thumbnail versions of the photos in the album as well as a toolbar containing useful buttons. See the detailed "Album Section," later in this section, for more information.

When running the software, a welcome screen (shown in Figure B-2) gives you a list of tasks that you can perform. These are actually the functions described throughout this guide and are not additional features.

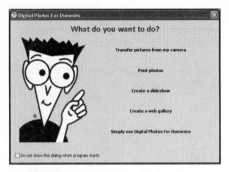

Figure B-2: A welcome way to begin.

Toolbar

The toolbar contains a whole host of different buttons, all of which will be active if you select an image.

These buttons include the main functions available in the menu, thereby providing you with quicker access. Here, we've matched each button with its corresponding function:

Button	*What It Does*
	Acquire images from the digital camera.
	Change from the Thumbnails to the Details display mode.

Button	***What It Does***
	Refresh the window display.
	Run the digital image retouching function.
	Convert from one format to another.
	Resize an image.
	Rotates counter-clockwise by 90°.
	Rotates clockwise by 90°.
	Starts a slideshow.
	Prints selected image.
	Starts the Help function.
	Exits the program.

Explorer

The Digital Photos For Dummies explorer screen contains two columns, as shown in Figure B-3. The first column displays the structure of the drives, folders, subfolders, and files on your system. The second column displays the contents of the elements selected in the first column.

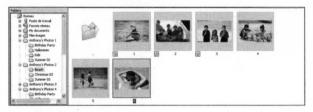

Figure B-3: The explorer only displays images and video files, and not the other file types.

To come to grips with this tool, browse through the folders containing images and you'll see them displayed as thumbnails. This is the default display mode, but you can choose not to display the thumbnails. To do so, simply click the second button in the toolbar.

If you prefer to use the Thumbnails display mode, you can change the different thumbnail sizes. To increase or reduce their size, use the + and – keys on your keypad.

Albums list

When you create and save photo albums, they appear in that window as a list. If you click on any album's name, it

opens in the Album section at the bottom of the window
(see the following section).

Album section

The top of the Album section contains a toolbar with 13
buttons. The Album section itself can be found right at
the bottom of the work screen. To create an album,
simply place the required photos inside the frame, as
shown in Figure B-4. To do so, you can drag-and-drop
them or you can even select the desired images and press
the * key on the keypad to transfer them.

You can select several images by holding down the Shift
key or the Ctrl key, as with all other Windows applica-
tions. The Shift key lets you select groups of photos,
whereas the Ctrl key lets you pick out the files here and
there.

Figure B-4: Creating your album by placing your images in the bottom
frame.

Here's the list of the 13 buttons in the Album section's
toolbar and their corresponding functions:

Button	*What It Does*
	Creates a new album. *Caution:* Save your current album before starting a new one. Creating a new album clears the current album.
	Loads an existing album.
	Saves an album.
	Deletes the current album.
	Deletes the selected photos from the album.
	Deletes all photos from the album.
	Copies all the photos in the current album to the Windows clipboard.
	Enables you to print photos individually or as a contact sheet.
	Displays images in the current album as a slideshow.
	Helps you to design a customized slideshow and configure options for it.

Button	*What It Does*
	Enables you to send the photos in your album via e-mail.
	Helps you to create a Web page based on the photos in your album.
	Resizes all or selected photos in your album.

Loading Photos from a Digital Camera

You may already have tons of images on your hard disk or on CD-ROMs that you want to work in Digital Photos For Dummies, and you can easily access those via the Explorer window. Yet at the same time, you may need to transfer the photos taken with your digital camera to your PC. Digital Photos For Dummies provides you with easy ways to gain access to your photos wherever they are.

Digital Photos For Dummies contains a utility for loading your photos directly from your camera, regardless of the make and model.

Running the configuration wizard

Before you can download your photos, the program has to recognize your camera. You only need to perform this procedure once:

1. **Click the Get Pictures button.**

   You see the Image Downloader dialog box.

   You have two ways to indicate what kind of camera you are working with. Do either Step 2a or Step 2b, whichever way works better for you.

2a. **Choose Tools⇨Options.**

   The Options dialog box appears, as shown in Figure B-5. In this dialog box, you choose your camera type, according to the connection used (camera brands are indicated after each connection type so you can choose the right one). The possibilities are:

   • **USB Auto-connect**

   • **Sierra Imaging USB**

   • **Sierra Imaging Serial**

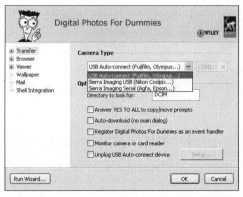

Figure B-5: Choose your connection (USB, and so on).

2b. **Click the Run Wizard button to launch the hardware configuration utility.**

The wizard automatically detects which type of camera you have. After confirming via the Next button, you see a screen where you have to specify the type of connection used by your camera.

3. **After the software can recognize your camera type, you have the opportunity to choose a destination folder for your downloaded pictures.**

4. **Finally, the wizard offers automatic picture renaming because the filenames that most cameras think of aren't very intuitive but just a series of meaningless numbers.**

Downloading digital photos

After completing the configuration wizard (as explained in the previous section), the program takes you to the Image Downloader dialog box where you can specify the type of action to be performed (Move or Copy) and the target directory for the photos to be transferred.

The difference between moving and copying images is that when you move images, the files are deleted from their original locations. When you copy images, on the other hand, the images remain in their original locations and are copied to the new locations.

You can also decide for yourself which photos are to be loaded by checking the Let Me Select Images to Download box. Then, after you click OK, the Select Images dialog box appears displaying a thumbnail of each image in the source directory.

You can also decide whether or not you wish to keep the original folder structure or keep all the files in the same folder. Simply select the Keep Directory Structure option in the Image Downloader dialog box to maintain the original structure or select the Flatten Directory Structure option to keep the pictures in one folder.

Finally, there are a few additional options, which are basically actions that the software does or doesn't perform after loading the photos. By default, the Close This Window box is checked, along with Browse Images. Other options include exotic stuff such as Fix Dead/Hot Pixels (removes small pixels that are defective on a digital camera), or transform image based on EXIF orientation tag (automatically orients your image to landscape or portrait mode according to the information embedded in the file when you took the shot with your digital camera). You can have fun playing with these after you get bored with the basics.

To locate the downloaded images, simply check out the Digital Photos For Dummies explorer and go to the target directory you chose for storing the images loaded from the camera.

Working with Albums

Digital Photos For Dummies has an effective tool for sorting, organizing, and storing your digital photos — the album. Albums enable you to select groups of images according to a theme, period, or any other category and put them together within a virtual album.

Choosing and adding images

Adding images to an album couldn't be simpler. Use the Digital Photos For Dummies explorer to open the directories containing the photos that you want to save in an album and then drag them to the Album section at the bottom of the explorer, as explained in the section "Album section," earlier in this chapter.

You can add as many images as you want from as many different directories as you want. After you finish adding pictures to your album, click the Save button (it looks like a diskette) on the toolbar at the top of the Album section. After you save the album with the name of your choice, you can go back to it at a later stage and change it by adding or discarding photos as needed. To do so, simply click on the load album button (the second icon in the Album toolbar).

Be sure to save your current album before starting a new one with the New Album button. Clicking the New Album button clears the contents of the Album area. If you haven't saved the album, your changes are lost.

Other buttons are available for emptying or actually deleting albums. For more information about the Album toolbar, see the section titled "Album section," earlier in this guide.

If you're not really sure how to categorize your photos, try dividing them by people or activities. That way, you end up with a vacation album that spans several years or an album reserved for a particular member of your family.

Making and viewing slideshows

One of the best features of albums, in addition to their functions for categorizing and archiving, is your ability to use albums to create custom slideshows. A slideshow is an animated presentation of your photos. Digital Photos For Dummies enables you to create as many slideshows from your albums as you wish.

A slideshow can be created from an album. The album doesn't necessarily have to be saved on your hard disk, but you must at least be in the process of editing it.

You can create a slideshow in a couple of ways:

> **Viewing the automatic slideshow:** By clicking the Slideshow button at the top of the album (it's the purple movie camera), you can watch an automatic slideshow of the pictures in the album.

> To modify the presentation of an automatic slideshow, choose Tools➪Options and expand the Viewer, Slideshow configuration directory on the left side of the Options dialog box. Then you can make general changes to the presentation of your slideshow, such as whether to use transitions and how long each image is displayed.

> **Building a custom slideshow:** You gain far greater control over your slideshow by building a custom slideshow rather than just viewing the automatic slideshow. A custom slideshow allows you to share your slideshow with friends and family via e-mail or on a CD-ROM. You can only build a custom slideshow from an album.

To build a custom slideshow, follow these steps:

1. **Order your photos.**

   Digital Photos For Dummies builds your custom
   slideshow in the same order that your images
   appear in the album, so you begin by dragging
   your images into the order you want.

2. **Click the Build Slideshow button.**

   This is the black movie camera in the Album
   area. The Build Slideshow dialog box appears,
   which enables you to create a highly personal
   piece of work with a definite multimedia feel to it.

3. **Choose the type of slideshow to be created.**

   Digital Photos For Dummies gives you a choice of
   three options:

   Standalone slideshow (EXE): This creates an exe-
   cutable file (EXE) that anyone can read on his or
   her computer. It's ideal for e-mailing or burning
   onto a CD and then handing out to your friends
   and family.

   Adobe Acrobat Slideshow (PDF): In this case,
   you'll need Adobe Acrobat Reader (free) to view
   the slideshow. Note that background music can't
   be added with this format.

   Windows Screensaver (SCR): With this format,
   you can create a screensaver that can be used
   directly by Windows. This is a good default
   option.

   You can also select an option called Build
   Autorun SlideShow. This creates an autorun file,
   which is executed as soon as the medium containing it (such as a CD-ROM) is inserted in the
   drive.

4. **Adjust the display settings.**

   The settings are described as follows:

   Delay: This value corresponds to the amount of time that each image is displayed on the screen.

   Action: Two options are available. The first one simply just converts the images into JPEG format to prevent the slideshow from taking up too much space. The second option allows you to resize the images and trim down the file size even more.

   Resize: This function is only available if you chose the second of the two options in the Action field. Specify the required size.

   JPEG Quality: Adjust the quality according to your requirements. Try out different settings and click the Preview button to see whether you've got the right level of quality.

   Total Size: This value indicates the size of your slideshow. To find out what it'll be after making a few changes, click the Refresh button.

   Number of images: This isn't a user-definable setting, but just information on the number of images used for the slideshow currently being created. If the number isn't correct, save the album to update the number.

5. **Choose transitions between images.**

   You can choose from a number of interesting transitions from one image to another. Digital Photos For Dummies has nearly a hundred transitions to choose from. To activate them, check the Use Transitions box and display the list of available transitions by clicking the Select button.

Simply check the boxes that you're happy with and the selected transitions are used randomly when your slideshow's images are presented.

You can also specify the transition duration. The value is expressed in seconds and may vary between 0.5 seconds and 99 seconds.

6. **Add background music.**

   Click the Background Music button and pick out the required file (Wave, WMA or MP3) from your hard disk. The track will be played over and over again, unless you interrupt the slideshow presentation.

E-mailing an album

Digital Photos For Dummies can optimize a series of images so that you can e-mail them. Just follow these steps:

1. **Click the Mail button.**

   It looks like an @ symbol. The first time that you do so, you are asked to configure your account details in the Options dialog box. The easiest thing to do is check the box at the top so that your main account (the one you use most often) will be used. Note that you only need to do this once. After you finish, the Send Pictures by Mail dialog box appears.

2. **Define the conversion and readjustment settings.**

   This allows you to minimize the size of your files for use in e-mail.

3. **Click the Send button.**

   All the photos in the current album are attached to a message in your e-mail program. Enter the recipient's address, stick in the subject line, and add some text if you want.

Transforming an album into a Web page

The Instant Web Gallery button, as its name suggests, lets you instantly create Web pages of your albums for use in your personal Web site.

Clicking the Instant Web Gallery button opens the Instant Web Gallery dialog box, which contains various ready-to-use pages, as well as some options and display settings (names displayed, image size, slideshow, and so on). *Caution:* It's not actually a Web page editor, but just a basic, though effective, creation tool. See the Help files in the software for more details about creating Web galleries.

Retouching Your Photos

Image retouching refers to the corrections that you can make and the special effects that you can add to your photos. In both cases, retouching may affect all or part of the edited image. Digital Photos For Dummies boasts a large number of editing tools that you can find out about in this section.

Basic corrections

Here's a series of corrections that you'll often need to make.

Rotating an image

Rotating an image couldn't be easier — the toolbar has all the functions for the job. Simply select the image or images that you want to straighten by clicking on it/them, and then orient by 90° clockwise or counter-clockwise as required.

To select multiple images to rotate, hold down the Ctrl key while clicking additional images.

Renaming an image

The name given to each of your photos is displayed beneath each thumbnail. The camera may have given the name to the picture, in which case the name looks more like a code than an explicit and descriptive name. To rename an image, select it, wait a second and then click once on the image's name. You can now enter the name of your choice.

Make sure you keep the file extension (such as .jpg or .bmp) when you rename a picture; otherwise, the program will no longer recognize the photo as an image and therefore will be unable to read or display the image. If you do accidentally delete the file extension, find the file using Windows Explorer and reassign the original file extension so that the program can read it again.

Enhance mode

Digital Photos For Dummies comes with a dedicated Enhance mode for the purpose of making structural corrections to your photos. You can access it in three ways:

- ✔ Select the photo to be modified and then click the Enhance button in the toolbar.

- ✔ Select the photo to be modified and then press Shift+E.

- ✔ Right-click on the image to be edited and choose Enhance from the pop-up menu that appears.

Choosing the display

The Enhance window offers you three display modes for your photo:

- ✔ **Before mode:** For displaying your photo in its initial state

- ✔ **Before & After mode:** For displaying the modified image alongside the original

- ✔ **After mode:** For displaying only the image being modified

Before & After mode, shown in Figure B-6, provides you with a continual means of checking the modified image against the original version. This gives you a real perspective of the changes you make.

Figure B-6: Before & After mode is extremely
practical for viewing your modifications.

Five tools at your service

The Enhance Image window provides five tools for
enhancing your images. You can find the tools on the
right-hand side of the window in the Select a Tool panel.

Depending on the tool that you select, the options in the
Configure the Tool panel are different. In order of appear-
ance, here are the five tools provided courtesy of Digital
Photos For Dummies.

Quick Fixes

Quick Fixes contains three functions for automatic adjust-
ments: Auto Levels (for adjusting the image's brightness),

Auto Contrast (for automatically adjusting the contrast), and Sharpen (for getting your image in sharper detail).

Auto Levels and Auto Contrast can only be applied once, following which they are grayed out, whereas the Sharpen function can be used several times in succession.

Brightness & Contrast

As its name suggests, this tool offers two settings — one to increase or reduce the image's brightness and the other to adjust the level of contrast for your photo. You can therefore correct over- or underexposed images and make out details that were previously hidden.

Saturation

Saturation determines the level of color contained in your image. Adjusting this setting to zero produces an image in grayscale. If you drastically increase the saturation, faint colors become much more pronounced.

Red Eye Removal

Red eyes are a common fault that mainly occurs when using the flash to take photos of people with blue eyes. Digital Photos For Dummies provides you with an accurate and effective tool for getting rid of the red-eye effect:

1. **Open the photo and enhance the image.**

   You can open the Enhance Image dialog box by using one of the three methods described in the section titled "Enhance mode."

2. **Zoom into the first eye to be corrected.**

   To do so, use the magnifying glass in the Miscellaneous Options panel at the bottom left of the Enhance Image window.

3. **Resize and reposition the selection area.**

   Do so in an After panel by adjusting the sizing
   handles on the sides and corners of the selection
   area, as shown in Figure B-7. To move the area,
   place your mouse in the top third of the selection
   area and drag the area. You need to be as accurate as possible when defining the selection area
   around the eye.

4. **Click the Apply button.**

   The pupil becomes black again. Repeat for entire
   process for other eyes to be adjusted.

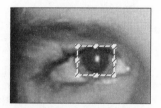

Figure B-7: Redefining the selection
area around a zoomed-in eye.

Crop & Borders

Sometimes you want to select just part of a photo or put
a border or frame around a photo to give it a fresh focus.
Again, Digital Photos For Dummies has the right tool for
the job — the Crop & Borders tool.

Cropping a photo is the digital way of cutting out the
important stuff, meaning that you can keep part of an
image and get rid of such things as an unnecessary out-
line. To crop an image, follow these steps:

1. **Open the photo and enhance the image.**

   You can open the Enhance Image dialog box by using one of the three methods described in the section titled "Enhance mode."

2. **Click the Crop & Borders button.**

3. **Position the selection area and resize it until it frames the area that you want to crop to.**

   Use the resizing handles on the corners and sides of the selection area to resize it. To move the area, place your mouse in the top third of the selection area and drag the area.

4. **Click the Apply button.**

   The photo is cropped to the area that you selected.

You can also crop the image by using the standard formats. To do so, choose one of the options corresponding to the standard photo formats from the Aspect Ratio menu. (See the Help files in the software for more details on how the Adjust Selection to Allow Lossless Cropping checkbox works.)

Adding a digital frame or border either just inside the edge or just outside the edge of your image is also a snap. Follow these steps to add a border:

1. **Open the photo and enhance the image.**

   You can open the Enhance Image dialog box by using one of the three methods described in the section titled "Enhance mode."

2. **Click the Crop & Borders button.**

   Note: When adding a border, you can safely ignore the cropping marks; the box doesn't affect what you are framing unless you actually apply the Crop tool.

3. **Click the Add Borders button so that the Borders dialog box appears.**

4. **Fill in the Borders dialog box to create the kind of border you want on your image.**

   You can choose to have an inner frame, a drop shadow, one or two outer frames, or any combination thereof. You choose the width and color of each border to set off your photo however you like. A Preview image lets you see how different framing options would look as you're deciding.

5. **Click OK when you're satisfied with the border.**

Confirming your choices

Whatever corrections you've just applied, you'll have to confirm them by clicking the Save button. If you're not sure, click the Cancel button and any modifications you've made to the photo will be ignored.

By default, Digital Photos For Dummies appends the word _Edited to photos that you have modified. This system keeps your original files intact. You can, of course, change the name to anything you like at this point.

Batch modifications

Suppose you need to rename or resize several photos (say, 100 or so) all at the same time. Batch modifications can help in a jiffy. As always, there are several ways to access these functions, one of which involves the use of the Advanced options in the Image menu. Here are some things you can do in batches:

✔ **Rename a series of photos:** Digital cameras tend to give pictures puzzling names by default, so you may find that you want to rename every picture coming from your camera. To save time you can make all your changes at once.

✔ **Resize a series of photos:** Have you taken a lot of photos, only to realize that they're all of different sizes? If identical sizes are what you want, then the Resize tool can help. You can adjust one or both dimensions of your photos, change the format (see the next bullet point), and preview the resulting file sizes before you commit to your choices.

✔ **Convert images from one format to another:** There are several graphic formats for images, such as JPG, BMP, and TIF. These formats differ from one another due to their rate of compression, the number of colors that they can support, and so on. Some are more useful for posting images on the Web, and others enable better quality printing.

With JPG, you can choose a level of quality (between 0 and 100) that determines the size-to-quality ratio of your converted image. The closer you get to 100, the better quality your image (though it takes up more space), and vice-versa.

Consult the Help files in the software for specific steps on how to use the batch modification tools.

Printing Photos

Digital Photos For Dummies offers you a range of different tools for printing your photos. You can print out just one photo, or you can adjust the page layout to print several different photos on the same page.

Printing just one photo

Select the photo that you'd like to print by clicking on it in the explorer. Then right-click and choose the Print function.

The Print Settings window opens and is divided into five sections (see Figure B-8). The first section, Choose the layout, prompts you to choose between Many images per page, One image per page, and a Contact sheet. The second section enables you to choose the quality of the printed images. The third lets you choose the orientation of the printed picture. The fourth lets you choose the format of printing paper you will use. The last one enables you to choose your printer.

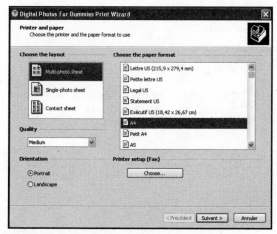

Figure B-8: Print options window.

Depending on the layout you choose, the next screen will offer different printing options, such as the brand and type of printing paper for multi-photo layout, the size and ability to scale and crop your single image, or the number of columns and rows on your contact sheet.

When all the settings appear correct, click the OK button to start printing.

Printing a contact sheet

The contact sheet is a medium frequently used by photo labs and professional photographers. It displays a series of miniature photos on one sheet and enables you to create an index so that you know what photos you have at a glance. To find out the detailed steps for creating your own contact sheet, consult the Help files in the software.

Printing an album

To print one or more photos from an album, simply open the album in question and then click the Print button in the Album section's toolbar.

The window displayed is none other than the main print window described in the previous section.

The advice and explanations you need to succeed

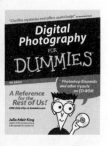
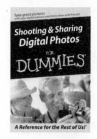

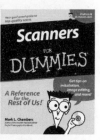

Look for these titles wherever books are sold, call 877-762-2974, or visit dummies.com.

Interactive software — as easy as ABC!

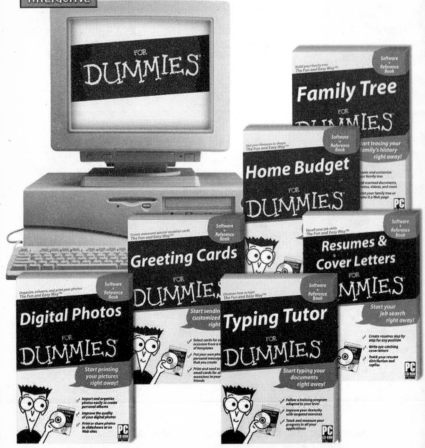

For more information or to order,
go to www.anuman-interactive.com

Anuman End-User License Agreement

By using this CD-ROM, you are implicitly agreeing to the following software license. If you disagree with the terms of this license, please return the product in its original packaging to the place where you purchased it.

The following provisions apply to the license and to the warranty. They constitute a legal contract ("License Contract") between you (as an individual or a legal entity) and Anuman Interactive, and its affiliated companies, governing the product and all the accompanying support, software and printed or online documentation. The software is licensed and not sold to you and its use is subject to this License Contract. Anuman Interactive grants you a limited, personal, non-exclusive license to use the software in the manner described in the user documentation.

The license covers all the files on the CD-ROM as well as the present documentation. The entity thus defined will be termed "the Product".

1. Total or partial reproduction of the Product by whatever means is prohibited. Any illegal copy will constitute an infringement of patent, prohibited by sections 425 ff. of the French Penal Code.

2. The Product shall be installed on one computer only, and exclusively for private use.

3. You may not sell (or even give) the user license for the Product to any other party.

4. The rights to the Product are the sole property of Anuman Interactive; they may not be sold or otherwise transferred to any other party.

5. The Product may not be rented, leased or lent out (even free of charge) or publicly displayed or otherwise distributed.

6. The Product may not be transferred from one computer to another or used on any communication network without explicit authorisation from the publisher.

7. The elements that make up the Product, and any documents produced by the acquirer with the aid of these elements, may not be used for commercial purposes.

8. The Product is supplied "as is". Anuman Interactive guarantees that the medium is free of any known defects for a period of ninety (90) days as from the date of purchase. This warranty excludes any dysfunction arising from misuse of the Product. The publisher's financial liability shall under no circumstances exceed the purchase price of the Product.

9. In no event will Anuman Interactive or its employees be liable for any incidental, indirect, special, consequential or punitive damages, or any damages whatsoever (including, without limitation, damages for injury to person or property, for loss of profits, business interruption, loss of business information, loss of privacy, failure to meet any duty and negligence) arising out of or in any way related to the use or inability to use the software, even if the company or an authorized representative of Anuman Interactive has been advised of the possibility of such damages.

10. The data contained in the Product are provided for information only; Anuman Interactive shall not be held liable for any error, omission, or oversight which may be encountered in the Product nor for the consequences, whatever they may be, arising from the use of the data provided.

11. The files on the CD-ROM, and the title of the Product, are the property of Anuman Interactive. This product is protected by copyright laws and by international copyright treaties.

12. Acquirers are entitled to technical support. Anuman Interactive provides through a local provider free technical support by telephone, fax, or e-mail.

13. This License is effective until terminated. You may terminate this License at any time by destroying the Product. This License will terminate automatically without notice from Anuman Interactive if you fail to comply with any provision of this License. All provisions of this License as to warranties, limitation of liability, remedies and damages will survive termination.

14. If any provision or portion of this License is found to be unlawful, void or for any reason unenforceable, it will be severed from and in no way affect the validity or enforceability of the remaining provisions of this License contract.